Scottish Towns

Scottish Towns

A GUIDE FOR LOCAL HISTORIANS

David Moody

B. T. Batsford Ltd · *London*

First published 1992

Typeset by Deltatype Ltd, Ellesmere Port
and printed in Great Britain by
Billings Ltd, Worcester

Published by B. T. Batsford Ltd
4 Fitzhardinge Street, London W1H 0AH

A catalogue record for this book is
available from the British Library

ISBN 0 7134 6497 6

CONTENTS

ILLUSTRATIONS

Clydebank around 1910 with John Brown's shipyard workers on the bridge over the Forth and Clyde canal. A photograph illustrating the symbiosis of working-class tenement, communication routes and industry. Industrial housing even doubles up as advertisement hoarding. Here the bow windows are rounded and used as a solution to the architectural problem of bevelling on a street junction.

ACKNOWLEDGEMENTS

For help in supplying illustrations and permission to reproduce them, grateful acknowledgements are due to: The Scottish Record Office; East Lothian District Library; and Brodies WS.

Detail from a steel engraving of Dundee harbour of 1841. By the
nineteenth century the vigorous simplicity of the copper used by Slezer
(see p.15) had been supplanted by the fine detail of the steel engraving, of
which hundreds were produced for sale in book form or as individual
plates. Dundee harbour, which at the turn of the century was a 'crooked
wall enclosing but a few smuggling or fishing craft', here features an
open wharf timber construction on wooden piles – typical of systematic
dock construction throughout the century until the advent of steel piles
and reinforced concrete. By that time Dundee had 3.5 miles of quayside –
in this print a network of inner and outer docks is already developing.

Chapter One

INTRODUCTION

'The expression "populous Place" shall mean any Town, Village, Place or Locality . . . containing a Population of Seven hundred Inhabitants or upwards' runs the preamble to the Police and Improvement (Scotland) Act 1862. Such places, the act continues, should be empowered to elect commissioners and magistrates with responsibility for policing, public health measures, lighting and building control. That a community of as few people as 700 was given the right to a self-governing town council with all the trappings of provosts' chains and coats of arms was in part a recognition of the distinctive character of Scottish settlements – small by neighbouring English standards, and often separated from other similar communities by an inhospitable terrain. It is interesting that in the Scandinavian countries of Denmark and Sweden, where in places similar conditions prevail, definitions of 'urban' for census purposes likewise adopt a small population base – in their case as low as 200.

No adequate definition of what constitutes a town has yet been widely accepted, though certain general elements – that the community be of 'some size', with significant non-agricultural employment and the presence of institutions – are common to most attempts. The difficulty in being more precise stems from the elusiveness of urbanism, and controversy as to the key factor behind the existence and growth of towns. There may indeed not be any one single factor, rather a coalescence of different types of human behaviour, which suggests that the phenomenon which we call a town may have a deep structural compatibility with our aspirations.

That it is the structure and not any geographical delineation which constitutes a town explains how a settlement of a few hundred people can evoke the same feelings of pride and affection as a city of a million, and makes it possible for a book of this kind to talk in common terms of the urbanism of cities such as Glasgow (population 744,000 in 1981) and Edinburgh (400,000) and of the successors of the small police burghs of the mid-nineteenth century (Ballater, for example, with a

1981 population of under 1,000). For despite the disparity of scale, there are numerous shared features. The Glasgow pattern of a medieval town core spreading outwards, with handsome mansions later converted into banks and offices, is commonplace. The Georgian domestic street grids of Edinburgh are reproduced in Paisley (83,000) but also in small burghs such as Blairgowrie (6,900). The existence of a high-prestige retail central district giving way rapidly to a low-status area of wholesaling, car parking, small-scale workshop industries and bus stations is common to large and small alike.

As well as similarity of structure, there is also similarity of content. Edinburgh's typical inner-city four-storey tenements of sandstone, complete with bay windows, and its equally typical stone-faced bungaloid suburbs on the rising slopes of Duddingston, are mirrored by a stray tenement block and half a road of bungalows in the small seaside burgh of North Berwick (4,700). Similarly the two towns share the Victorian stone villa and terrace, the cottage council house of the 1920s and 1930s and the ubiquitous two-up, two-down council version of the traditional tenement. Despite the distinct individuality of the smaller town, it is in some respects a miniature version of the larger. 'All towns are alike in some respects, and unlike in others', suggest Fraser and Sutcliffe (1983), and this book hopes to suggest some ways of exploring this paradox.

Though large cities have existed since Sumerian times, if not before, the urbanization which we know today is a phenomenon of the last two hundred years. At the beginning of the nineteenth century, Scotland's population was over-whelmingly rural (80–90 per cent). The mid-century was a milestone, in that the percentage in urban centres (defined as settlements of in excess of 2,000 population) had passed 50 per cent. By 1891 the proportion of those in towns was 65.4 per cent. The figure for 1981 is 89.1 per cent (the definition of a rural centre being a settlement under 1,000).

A corresponding trend has been a disproportionate growth in the size of the four main cities of Aberdeen, Dundee, Edinburgh and Glasgow, which together accounted for only 11 per cent of the Scottish population in 1801. Glasgow, with a population of 33,500 in 1755, boasted 658,000 inhabitants in 1891, a figure which jumped to over a million with the incorporation of some of its suburban burghs shortly afterwards. Between 1901 and 1951, the four cities accounted for between 38 per cent and 46 per cent of the population. The areas covered by the cities also grew enormously. Glasgow's size increased in the nineteenth century from 715 to 5,134 hectares, an increase all the more remarkable in that the city was at the same time the most densely populated in Britain, with 700,000 people in three square miles in 1914.

Urbanization was not restricted to the four major cities, as the table below indicates. The 1755 figures are the estimates for the burghal parishes taken by Dr Webster:

	1755 (nearest 100)	1891 (nearest 1,000)	1981 (nearest 1,000)
Paisley	6,800	66,000	83,000
East Kilbride	2,000*	3,800*	70,000
Motherwell and Wishaw	5,600†	34,000	67,000
Greenock	3,900	63,000	58,000
Irvine	4,000	9,000	55,000
Clydebank	2,700**	10,000	52,000
Coatbridge	4,500††	30,000	51,000
Dunfermline	8,600	22,000	51,000
Hamilton	3,800	25,000	51,000
Kilmarnock	4,400	28,000	51,000

*Kilbride parish †Dalziel, Hamilton & Cambusnethan parishes
**Kilpatrick East & West parishes ††Monklands East & West parishes

These are the largest towns, and several more have populations in excess of 40,000 (Airdrie, Ayr, Bellshill, Cumbernauld, Johnstone, Kirkcaldy and Perth).

The scale of this transformation does not reflect merely an overall increase in population. It represents also a depopulation of rural areas – a movement of population from scattered farm towns around what are today's steadings to nucleated settlements (villages and towns). Those areas of Scotland where village and town formation have been sparse (such as the Highlands) have actually suffered a net loss of people (three and a half per cent between 1901 and 1971) despite the growth of a town such as Inverness from 9,700 in 1755 to 34,800 in 1971.

For the local historian, the most important consequence to

grasp is that the town he or she studies today is almost entirely a creation of the nineteenth and twentieth centuries. Structurally, the central core may date back as far as the middle ages, but the core represents only a tiny proportion of the surface area of today's town. Architecturally, even the core is recent in date, for the individual buildings, or at very least their frontages, have been reconstructed. Even Edinburgh's famous Royal Mile tenements are almost all nineteenth- and twentieth-century buildings. The intention of this book is to look at ways of studying the visual impact of the towns we inhabit today; it will therefore concentrate on the recent features we find about us – our homes, shops and places of work – rather than the exceptional historic buildings which have been preserved.

Lewis Mumford in his panoramic *The City in History* (1961) talked of the uncouth disorder of the modern town, but others have been kinder. Donald Olsen (1983) found that 'many of us feel a kind of protective affection even for cities that are by any standards ugly. The valuable thing about all cities is that they bring people together, and bring them together in a way different from and better than other artificial concentrations of humanity'. Lawrence Saunders in his study of the pioneering period of the Scottish industrial town (1950) makes a similar point in emphasizing the freedom of choice which urban living bestows: 'Each component individual would be enabled to become a person, enlightened, responsible, enjoying a wide range of satisfactions that were independent of such accidents as birth and rank and material circumstance.'

Diversity of individual expression is a key characteristic of the existing fabric and structure of towns. Mumford may rail against their uniformity, against their dependence on economic forces – typified by the rectangular land blocks of the business developer, blocks which 'can be most simply reduced to standard monetary units for purchase and sale'; and against their suburbs as 'a multitude of uniform, unidentifiable houses lined up inflexibly, at uniform distances on uniform roads'. The forces which produce these results are real enough. But that framework also encompasses, like masons' marks on history, the strivings, the eccentricities, the ideals, mediocre or otherwise, of builders, architects, politicians, entrepreneurs, dreamers and (most importantly) inhabitants who individually and communally have created the social fabric just as church spires and, more recently, office and apartment blocks have determined the physical outline of the townscape.

'I too am sentimental about ugliness' says a character in Saul Bellow's novel *Humboldt's Gift* of urban squalor; and Professor Checkland in his study of Glasgow (1976) talks, in contrast to Mumford's 'uncouth disorder of the industrial town' of the city's new road system 'making visible the excitement of an industrial landscape and its setting of encircling hills'. This exciting jumble of human excellence, mediocrity and greed may be brought into focus by consideration of its antithesis – those offspring of autocrats known as planned villages, of which numerous examples were built in the late eighteenth century. Aesthetically, such villages can be delightful, but to look at rather than to live in as far as the convinced town dweller is concerned. The unity of their inspiration lacks the stimulus that comes from the juxtaposition of conflicting ideals and interests. As historical monuments preserved in amber, they lack one exciting historical perspective – the impinging of the buildings of one age upon those of another, whether sympathetic or otherwise. Their nearest modern equivalents in the planning sense, the new towns of East Kilbride, Glenrothes, Cumbernauld, Livingstone and Irvine, also provoke ambivalent sentiments. Adams (1978) celebrates Cumbernauld as a resurrection of the old Scottish burgh with its 'town centre rising grey like a dreadnought on the hilltop'; but residents have complained of 'new town neurosis' or 'new town blues', albeit most observers have seen this as a temporary, 'transitional' state (Higgs, 1977).

Ugliness is of course subjective, particularly in regard to the industrial environment. Early factory buildings inspired a generation of artists and attracted the attention of famous architects such as the country-house designer William Burn, who built the gas works beside the Water of Leith. The power to thrill of warehouses, railway tunnels and factory chimneys (including monumental designs such as James Maclaren Cox's 'Stack' in Dundee) has been attributed to the aesthetic of the sublime, fed by emotions of astonishment, awe and terror. The sublime reached its apogee in the mid-nineteenth-century Gothic revival, particularly the Venetian favoured by Ruskin, and was found not only in churches but in Glasgow's Stock Exchange and in what Taylor (1973) calls the 'basilisk glare across Glasgow Green of Templeton's Carpet Factory'. Elsewhere, in its elegant and awesome structures of cast iron and glass (in shopping malls, covered markets and railway stations), Victorian architecture found a true original voice. The monumental found new expression in the stark austerity of the inter-war style, with buildings such as the Art Deco St Andrews House in Edinburgh and Aberdeen's Bon Accord Baths. Of the former, McKean and Walker (1983) have noted the 'brooding, authoritarian characteristics' indicative of the 'secure headquarters of an occupying power'. That modern essay in the monumental – the tower block – has proved equally controversial.

Perhaps what our towns demand most of their inhabitants, and of local historians in particular, is a personal and emotional response to their anarchic eclecticism. 'We make our buildings and they make us' said Winston Churchill. The views of architectural historians about the bewildering succession of building styles vary so considerably that no acceptable aesthetic criteria can be too forcefully offered. Instead one can marvel at the diversity of human expression that has led many a small burgh to sport a Greek temple posing as a Calvinist church or a school, a Renaissance palace as a bank or an Egyptian tomb as a factory gatehouse.

Visual sources

An obvious and most immediate source for the study of towns is prints and photographs. 'Sometimes a picture is actually worth a thousand words', says Bruce Stave (1983), 'and the extensive employment of photographs to elaborate upon urban themes is not only appropriate but shows the need for many more volumes devoted to the photography of the city.' The surviving number is quite surprising – even the smallest burgh can boast hundreds, if not thousands. What is equally interesting is the selectivity in the choice of views. Main streets, big houses, pretty cottages have always had high symbolic value, sometimes unconsciously felt by the artist and photographer, and perhaps more consciously understood by commercial postcard producers. What we find much more rarely, therefore, are photographs of industrial sites, back streets (except those of the 'olde worlde' variety), suburbs, council estates and so on. The lesson is a valuable one for today's would-be recorder of the local environment. A systematic survey should include all aspects of a town, whether photogenic or otherwise.

Art and accuracy contending in this view of Ayr from Slezer's *Theatrum Scotiae* of 1693, with the town Kirk of St John the Baptist, as in many burghs, on a spacious out-of-town site. The riverside location, later to be exploited industrially for tannery and abattoir, is typical of the traditional burghs, many of which are represented for the first time in Slezer's collection. Also common is the sub-urb on the opposite bank – in Ayr's case a separate burgh.

Street views and panoramas executed from neighbouring vantage points have been part of the artistic heritage of towns since the seventeenth century. Warner (1983) suggests that their popularity was 'derived from public pleasure, if not direct merchant patronage, in seeing their city's buildings drawn and painted'. Edinburgh apart, the palm for the first substantial series of Scottish urban engravings goes to John Slezer, who worked in the second half of the seventeenth century (he was engineer to Charles II in Scotland). His most famous set was the *Theatrum Scotiae* of 1693, featuring numerous towns, though both the precision of his recording and the accuracy of his draughtsmanship have been called into question.

A burgeoning tourist market prompted the production of most of the engravings of the following century and a half, such as Robert Forsyth's five-volume *The Beauties of Scotland* (1805–8) and Joseph Swan's *Select Views of Glasgow and Its Environs* (1829). The arrival of mass-market steel engravings (following their predecessors on wood and copper) helped to broaden the range to include more urban scenes, such as those included in William Beattie's *Scotland Illustrated* (1838). These proponents of the British topographical school have left what have been described as 'attractive, clean, clear-cut vistas (no doubt somewhat idealized) of the later-Georgian and very early-Victorian city' (Best, 1973). They had, however, few followers, leaving a gap in the visual record of towns until the late nineteenth century.

Early photographers continued in the artistic tradition of the picturesque. Many indeed began (and even continued) as painters, for example William Young (1845–1916) from Catrine in Ayrshire and George Washington Wilson (*c*.1823–93). The latter began in the 1850s to offer his Aberdeen clients a choice between having their portraits painted, or being photographed. Wilson's landscape photographs developed in response to tourist demands for souvenirs and included the popular stereoscopic views. Competition came from English pioneers such as Francis Frith (1822–98) (who set himself the task of photographing every city, town and village in the British Isles), Francis Bedford, and William Lawrence, and the Scottish firm of James Valentine of Dundee. All were probably lesser photographers than Wilson, and it was a standing joke in his family that Valentine's essays so closely echoed his that his photographers 'must have used the same tripod holes to achieve their results' (Taylor, 1981). Postcard publishers of later generations have similarly stood on each others' toes.

The trend was towards commercialization. Taylor considers that 'the work of the 1880s and 1890s comes largely from second and third generation photographers who followed the visual traditions established by their predecessors but did not possess the deeper understanding that an artistic training would have given them'. Their numbers by this time were certainly substantial: the 1891 census lists 1,826 working photographers, a figure which excludes an additional number of part-time professionals, not to mention some famous amateurs such as Lady Henrietta Gilmour Montrave. Technical developments contributed, for the introduction of dry plate to replace wet-collodion in the 1880s made travel lighter for the photographer. Descriptions of the heroic expeditionary quality of early photographic trips brings an extra dimension to the appreciation of the beautiful prints the pioneers produced.

The change in emphasis has also been related to the more confident swagger of the first generation born to an urban existence and 'familiar with factories, lamplight, piped water, shop windows crammed with attractive luxuries and the clatter and bustle of "progressive" commerce-oriented life . . .' (Wilson, 1985). The subject matter of photographs accordingly changed. Listed in George Washington Wilson's catalogues at the end of the century were hotels, hydros, town halls, libraries, markets, railway stations, docks and even cemeteries – reading like 'an inventory of the town's buildings and local curiosities'. When Wilson's business went into liquidation at the start of the twentieth century, it had in stock 45,000 glass plate negatives. Frith's stock in 1914 was 52,000.

Changes in subject matter were accelerated by the development of the printed picture postcard, which ousted the photographic print from the mass market through its cheaper and much faster method of reproduction (the high quality half-tone printing process). Those firms (such as Wilson's) which stood by the traditional process went to the wall; those (such as Valentine's) which adopted the new technology, were more likely to thrive.

The first postcards appeared in 1870, when the Post Office introduced a plain white card which could be sent at half the letter rate. They were an instant success, with 76 million sold in the year. Postcards fulfilled the need now met by the telephone. With the Post Office wishing to preserve such a lucrative monopoly, non–official picture postcards could be sent only at full postal rate, and no writing was allowed on the plain side except the name and address – any brief message had to be scrawled across the front. In 1894 these cards were permitted to be sent at cheap rate, and in 1897 the restriction on the written message was abolished. These innovations, together with the later ones of the dividing line along the centre of the back (1902) and the front completely covered by the view without a white margin (also around 1902) help to date postcards accurately. Postmarks of course give a latest date: they could be many years old when bought or sent, and many publishers in fact touched up old views for reuse to save the bother of sending out a photographer.

Relaxation of the restrictions led to an explosion in the number of cards. The Edwardians carried bundles with them wherever they went 'and posted them upon the slightest provocation' suggests Byatt (1978). The scale of the phenomenon can be gauged by the fact that Millar and Lang of Glasgow, one of the foremost firms in the Edwardian age, published during 1904 one million cards per week. Other prominent Scottish enterprises were George Stewart & Co., Edinburgh (one of the pioneers of picture postcards with their sets of Edinburgh views in the 1890s), Willian Lyon of Glasgow (identified by the trademark 'Premier Series' on their cards), William Ritchie & Sons, Edinburgh (who produced the 'Reliable' series together with their trademark 'W.R.& S') and W. & K. Johnston Ltd of Edinburgh. There were of course also many major English publishers who produced Scottish cards – Raphael Tuck & Sons Ltd for instance.

Many cards appear to be the work of small local stationers and photographers. Some small town businesses, for example Brown & Co. of Lanark, worked throughout Scotland, and some others on a county basis (C. Reid of Wishaw, G. Bruce of Haddington). But most usually such cards were the work of large-scale firms who had negotiated a local franchise. The tell-tale 'printed in Germany' often indicates the nature of the operation, as most of the mass-produced cards emanated from that country.

Of the vast number of cards, not all by any means were topographical, though some businesses, such as Valentine's, did specialize in the view card. The golden age lasted until

1918 when the postage rate was doubled to one penny. Thereafter – and coincident with the spread of the postcard's rival, the telephone – many fewer millions were produced, though the number remained and still remains substantial. Most public and private collections will therefore probably feature in most depth the period roughly 1900–18 and can be dated from the Edward VII or George V postage stamp or the '½d rate' printed into the unused postage square.

In assessing the value of pictorial sources, postcards score low on evocation and social interest, but higher on topographical accuracy than many artistic photographs. That photographs can be misleading may seem odd, but they can be as inaccurate as the earlier artists' engravings, with buildings altered or omitted for aesthetic effect. Francis Frith would intensify areas of light and shade and remove 'unimportant' details; and would even superimpose two negatives of the same location for artistic ends. George Washington Wilson created dark foregrounds by shifting the camera lens to a position in which it was unable to cover the plate completely, thus leaving a section unexposed. Even Thomas Annan, famous through his depictions of the old closes and streets of Glasgow in 1868 and 1877 as the first great exponent of the art of documentary camera, 'added clouds, which brighten the skies over Glasgow's slums and . . . whitened the wash on the line. He did this for pictorial effect, for nice balance' (Mozley, 1977).

Expressive creativity and a response to the atmosphere of urban life tend to be missing from later topographical photographers, with their somewhat bland celebration of civic worthiness. There are of course exceptions. William Graham of Springburn (1845–1914), who was possibly dismissed from his job as an engine driver with the North British Railway in 1893, earned a professional living from photography for his last 11 years. In the words of Maurice Lindsay (1987) he 'brought into the focus of his camera everything from carthorses to cathedrals, from churches to rich mansions, street scenes and shops; above all, through people, apparently recording the despair and destitution with the same objectivity as the pomp of civic dignity'. Three thousand glass negatives are held by Glasgow District Library.

Unexpected finds of both amateur and professional work seem to have been the order of the day in recent years; and exhibitions and publications have promoted the long-unseen images of distinctive talents such as W. F. Jackson, Dr Francis Gray Smart and Thomas Begbie. Begbie's is a particularly early collection of glass negatives of Edinburgh and district from the 1850s, showing townscapes quite different from the familiar high-Victorian views to which we are used.

If some distortions result from the interpretations of photographers, others are due to our own prejudices. Donnachie & Macleod (1979) warn local historians against turning visual evidence into 'a propaganda exercise in the tradition of "gloom, grime and girning"; or to produce a trivialization . . . with plates of elderly "characters" whereas in fact the populace was predominantly youthful and vigorous. . . . Life in general was always far rougher and coarser than most collections can suggest'. With its patronizing attitude, the sepia disease which attacks local historians as well as the general public does a disservice to the past. The past is not a ready-made heritage museum, but was a serious business of earning a living, bringing up families and exploiting economic resources, just as life is today. A case in point is what we see as the photogenic horse and cart, which was no more photogenic to our ancestors than Ford Escorts are to us. Aldcroft (1982) points out that 'the stench and filth arising from the use of horses in city streets was probably as obnoxious and detrimental to public health, if not more so, as anything created by the motor vehicle'. The noise of juggernauts is no greater than that of horseshoe on cobblestone, whilst the dung and 10,000 or so carcasses of horses worked to death in an average British city in one year were a breeding ground of flies and an indirect source of cholera, typhoid fever, dysentery and infant diarrhoea. No wonder the advent of the motor car was hailed as the beginning of a new era of quiet and cleanliness.

Research ideas

Nearly all of us now live in towns of one kind or another, but in a large measure we do so unconsciously; unconscious, that is, of the myriad jumble of meanings in the local environment. The human geography of our artificial or man-made settlements is full of symbolism, reflecting mental patterns from the past. Because we are surrounded by the concrete expression of these meanings in the public preservation of the past in the present, we can refine our response to the symbols and become discoverers of meaning in the local townscape. A simple example is the wooden porchways of a semi-detached house or villa, for the builder or original occupier perhaps a conscious evocation of the Tudor age and all which that connotes of a rural (and mainly English) past, filtered muddily through the ethos of the Arts and Crafts movement of the beginning of this century. A local historian can benefit greatly by looking from the standpoint of an architectural historian.

A human settlement is also a series of spaces, not only in an absolute sense, but as an experienced subjective response. Such a view of space for instance dictates our perception of what constitutes a neighbourhood – after all, the boundaries are not marked on the ground. Certain features and buildings are key reference points of the mental map, giving them an importance out of all proportion to the ostensible function they may perform. Demolition of such buildings may provoke an unaccountable feeling of loss. Mental spaces help to explain the widespread feeling (though denied by some) that each town has a 'personality' which can be captured by the sensitive observer. This group of ideas fits into the discipline of the sociology of towns, or urban sociology, which is another important method of understanding urban life.

The arrangement of a town's space can also be considered in an absolute structural sense, which is a traditional concern of geography. Historical geography specializes in the study of changes in town layout over time, particularly in the context of economic developments.

The diversity of urban studies is a result of the varied input of these different academic disciplines. Asa Briggs suggests (1968) that the historian of the town 'not only requires the same gifts as other historians – analytical power, imagination, and a real sense of the past. He must also be a historian of something else besides . . . – of families, business, social and political movements, buildings, and of cultures and styles'.

The antiquarians who wrote their civic histories in the latter half of the nineteenth century, once the astonishing transformation of towns had completed its first phase, were too close to the events themselves to recognize general patterns in the growth of towns. The best of their work is full of local incident and anecdote, with miscellaneous data about people, streets and closes not obtainable from primary historical sources. It was sociologists such as Weber and Durkheim who began to suggest common characteristics and effects of urbanism, based on the view that 'there are a number of interesting and important differences between people in outlook and behaviour, according to whether their origin is rural or urban' (Schnore, 1968). The Chicago School of sociologists in the 1920s proposed a biological model of towns, seeing their growth as analogous to that of living organisms. More recently, sociologists have turned to more pragmatic questions about the way people behave in towns – how social and ethnic groups relate to each other, and how they are affected by local political decisions.

Sociologically inspired studies provide a necessary corrective to the tendency of geographers and architects to study the form of towns to the exclusion of the inhabitants. Talking of Scottish tenement life, one historian of Scottish housing remarked that 'the carriage of water, wash-day habits, the proximity of neighbours, children's games, the location of retailing outlets and shopping patterns all acquired a different significance when viewed from three or four flights of stairs' (Rodger, 1983). Some town dwellers – such as those on 'red Clydeside' – drew extreme conclusions from the differences between classes in the exploitation of urban space, and their analyses are supported by many modern historians, who claim that 'British towns of the industrial revolution were the conscious creation of the middle class, and the sources of their political and economic power' (Fraser & Sutcliffe, 1983). Oral history recording can get to the heart of people's views and experiences of urban living, and is one of the really worthwhile ventures for local historians. As a model of technique and achievement, one can point to Paul Thompson's published contributions, such as his *Voices from Within* (1973).

The historical study of towns obviously overlaps with geographers' interests. Their specialisms, such as urban geography and even urban historical geography as well as the more recent social geography, have contributed much to a theoretical understanding. One subject which has received a lot of attention and can easily be pursued by local historians, notwithstanding its abstruse name, is economic morphology – the changing character of different districts and suburbs. The balance of classes, races and their types of employment alters, imperceptibly in the short term, as does the use of buildings. Census enumeration books and valuation rolls allow such detailed history of streets to be reconstructed. Geography and economic history have almost merged into one in the last 50 years, economic factors being crucial for an understanding of town development. Studies range from the very descriptive traditional human geography (an analysis of a town's food supply or its retailing catchment area) to those analysing their common geometry.

An example of the latter is central place theory, which attempts to explain the business activity of a town in the wider context of its relationship with nearby towns. The theory suggests that both their size and distribution occur according to a fixed pattern (albeit modified by local geographical conditions). Each settlement has its catchment area, the smaller nested or enmeshed within those of larger settlements, according to the services which they provide. 'High order' goods such as furniture, fashion, clothing, needed at infrequent intervals, are part of the large hinterlands of cities and the like; 'low order' goods, which consumers will not travel large distances to acquire (such as food, banking, dry cleaning) are supplied at the most local level of settlement, whether suburb or small neighbouring town. The resulting geometry resembles a honeycomb.

The position of any settlement within the central place honeycomb matrix is important in an understanding of how the settlement grows. An example is Edinburgh, which from as early as the seventeenth century dominated the occupational structure of the surrounding burghs of Bo'ness, Dalkeith, Grangepans, Leith and Musselburgh, where there was a deficiency of professional and mercantile classes and a higher than normal proportion of a manufacturing and low level service workforce. Edinburgh also fits well into the theory of a 'primate' city, which posits that a country's leading urban area is disproportionately large and other towns are smaller and more numerous, by regular mathematical progression. Ironically, it was the absence of such a spread (thought so desirable for economic expansion) that lead to the deliberate foundation of many Scottish towns and villages in the late eighteenth and early nineteenth centuries, only for the founders to discover in many cases that the roots of economic expansion were somewhat more complicated. A caveat for local historians arising from these geographical studies is to avoid undue parochialism in the study of one's own town – its welfare and development is closely dependent upon what is happening in other settlements near and far.

Structural studies have considered not only spatial aspects but also the internal dynamics of towns. Frederick Engels, Karl Marx's collaborator, found that 'every fragment of disarray, every inconvenience, every scrap of human suffering has a meaning. Each of these is inversely and ineradicably related to the life led by the middle classes, to the work performed in the factories and to the structure of the city as a whole' (quoted by Marcus, 1973). A present day structuralist would agree, though with perhaps more emphasis on cultural and less on political meanings.

A more pragmatic political stance has introduced the idea of 'gatekeepers', managers intermediate between central government and processes operating at local level, in the towns themselves. The gatekeepers direct the allocation of scarce resources and decide who is to benefit from amenities. An example which is often cited is the routing of urban trunk and ring roads which, like their railway predecessors, more often than not pass through working-class housing areas. Gatekeeping is a function of both business and local authority interests. Studies of the local government of towns over the last 150 years are surprisingly few, despite the fact that a large part of the infrastructure, amenity and housing of all towns, as well as schooling and social services, are a direct result of its activities. The last chapter of the book is devoted to this subject.

Some standard sources

The reports of the decennial censuses are an easy to use and readily accessible published source. Separate volumes of county and large burgh reports were produced from 1911, before which time they are contained within the collection of Scottish volumes. The amount of statistical information included can be illustrated by a few examples.

The notoriously bad housing standards of the nineteenth and early twentieth centuries can be studied through the sections on overcrowded accommodation. In 1861, 43 per cent of the population in Inverness lived in apartments of no more than two rooms; even in 1911, 25 per cent lived in two rooms and 6.1 per cent in one room. Semi-rural Inverness is far from being the worst example. The principal occupations of the town's workforce are broken down into minute detail. In Dundee in 1841 a massive 50.5 per cent of the labour force was employed in textiles and clothing, with an even higher peak of 61.8 per cent in 1871. Alongside the sweep of such figures however, we also have specific information on the numbers of Dundee sweetmakers, newsboys, bill posters, ginger beer makers, bar men, gas workers and scavengers. Housebuilding troughs and peaks in response to the expansion and contraction of industry are shown by the number of building workers – 7.9 per cent of Aberdeen's workforce in 1881, declining to 4.7 per cent in 1911. Each report also contains a list of the principal institutions – poorhouses, barracks, hospitals, together with the numbers of inmates and staff. Emuneration books (the raw material on which the census analysis is based) even list the names of individuals.

Detail apart, the census returns can illuminate more general trends of urban development. One example is the decline in the urban mortality rate in the second half of the nineteenth century. The natural inclination is to attribute the decline to advances in sanitation, but a closer scrutiny reveals a more complex picture. For the lowering of the death rate was caused solely by extended longevity. Infant mortality levels by contrast remained constant and high. Comparative studies can be equally illuminating, showing for instance the substantially higher mortality rates in Victorian Dundee compared with the other large cities. Gordon (1985) attributes the difference to the low and irregular pay in the dominant textile industries, which reduced 'affordable nutritional and accommodation standards to such minimal levels as to expose large numbers of workers, and weaken their resistance, to environmental diseases'.

There will hardly be a burgh in Scotland that has not at some time promoted a local act of parliament for the introduction or improvement of a facility. Indeed, the major cities took great pride in pre-empting national legislation with their own tailored acts for the provision of police, water supply and power over slum clearance. The small burghs were often slow to follow, with the result that sanitary conditions were still appallingly primitive at the turn of the twentieth century. Sponsorship of local legislation in such towns was not concerned with the great environmental and social issues but with the improvement of transportation or communications, such as the financing of a new harbour or road. Private companies – gas, railway and so on – could similarly present local bills to parliament. For many facilities, an alternative and faster route was through application to the sheriff court, which Best (1968) calls the 'Pooh-Bah of Scottish local administration'. Sheriff court records are thus an important source, particularly their plan collections, now mostly in the Scottish Record Office. Bye laws adopted for the administration of national acts of parliament needed no statutory approval until the end of the century. In other areas, where the costly and time-consuming procedure for promoting local legislation was acknowledged (especially in new technology such as electricity supply and tramways which provoked a rush of applications), the device of the provisional order, submitted by the local authority to the Secretary for Scotland (later Secretary of State for Scotland) was introduced. Copies of local acts and provisional orders are common in public library local history and archive collections.

Local newspapers are abundant from Victorian times, being established even in burghs of 2,000 population upwards (one of the smallest appears to be the *Kingussie Record and Badenoch Advertiser*, founded in 1902, when the burgh numbered 989 inhabitants). That such a venture should be commercially viable is witness to the vitality of small communities – Adams (1978) talks of their 'communal heritage which cannot be reproduced within the city' and suggests that 'amid the national preoccupation with urban problems . . . the vitality of these small communities has often been forgotten'. Twenty per cent of Scotland's people still inhabit small towns. The Victorian foundation of local newspapers is also indicative of the intense participation of the middle classes in the infant local democracy of the time. The franchise was extended to all the middle class and some of the working class males in this period, and as one would expect, the former, in the guise of the industrial, landowning and religious leaders, dominated the various elected boards – for schooling, poor relief and sanitation. Their meetings and debates are reported almost verbatim in the local press, even down to the jeers, boos and applause, together with the vitriolic correspondence.

Then as now, the local paper also featured a mass of advertisements and a wealth of social information on balls and dinners, amateur dramatics, church news, the opening of buildings, employment and unemployment, sport and the activities of local societies. From the First World War, advertising came to oust other matters which had fought for space and attention – national and international news at second

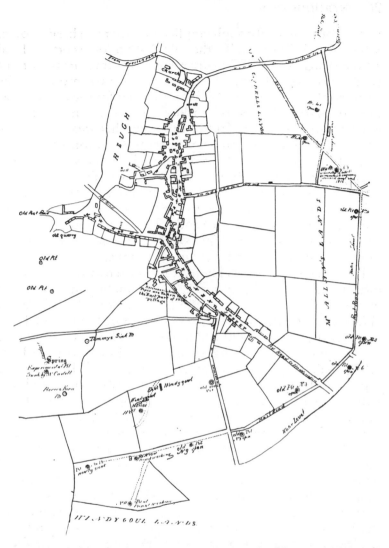

An estimated 30,000 plans were produced in Scotland between 1740 and 1850, in connection with court processes for the division of runrig, and rapid developments in roads, railways, bridges and other engineering works. The largest collection is now held in West Register House. For many towns, non-royal burghs in particular, their (often incidental) appearance on these plans is the only pre-Ordnance Survey representation ever made. Shown here is a part (slightly enhanced) of Plan of Tranent 1831 – evidence in a court action by the townspeople against the local coal entrepreneur Cadell, who, in sinking new shafts, had dried up the town's wells. The vaguely delineated central area and the square-field formation up to the back doors are indications that this is a burgh of barony, not a royal burgh.

hand and the serialized melodrama. Despite the small print (many newspapers consisted of only one large four-page leaf), such is their fascination that a problem for many researchers is to concentrate on a chosen subject without constant digression.

Commissions of inquiry set up by municipalities to report on grave social and industrial problems are local examples of the more common royal commission, government department and select committee of parliament inquiries established to carry out national surveys and make recommendations. The latter however are far from lacking in local interest, particularly those restricted to Scotland. Dr William Hutton Forrest, for example, who was medical attendant to the Stirling dispensary, describes in his submission (in the Reports on the Sanitary Condition of the Labouring Population of Scotland, 1842) how the poor throw their filth 'without any ceremony or hindrance from their windows into the public streets and closes'. Such graphic detail is one of the great strengths of these reports, whose style and content approximate not at all to the dullness popularly associated with official publications. Most of the important inquiry reports have been reprinted in the last twenty years, and researchers should be able to get their hands on reference copies through their public libraries.

The mapping of towns

The Ordnance Survey annual report for 1891 proudly boasted that the whole of urban Britain had been finally surveyed, at a scale 'sufficiently large to show detail down to the size of a doorstep'. Nothing further needs to be said to indicate the incomparable value of maps.

Systematic mapping of Scotland had begun at a scale of six inches to a mile (1:10560) in the 1850s – a far cry from doorstep representation. The whole country was to be mapped at this scale over the next thirty years. A 25 inch survey (1:2500) was authorized in 1854 and this series too was successfully completed during the century (except for uncultivated areas, which were excluded). Decisions over mapping at larger scales proved less consistent. Three different series were initiated mid-century for urban areas, at five feet to the mile (1:1056), ten feet to the mile (1:528) and at 1:500, which was a close approximation to the ten feet scale. A criterion

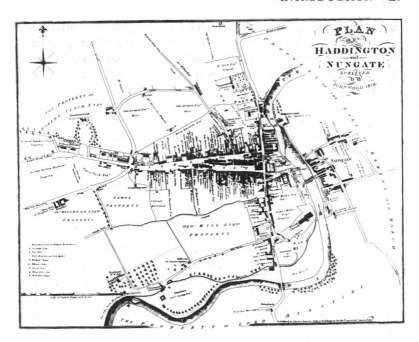

Plan of Haddington from James Wood's *Town Atlas of Scotland*, 1828, one
of the best sources of pre-Ordnance Survey mapping. Smaller and more
schematic are the 75 burgh plans of 1832 to establish electoral boundaries
for the reformed parliamentary constituencies. Haddington town centre
shows a typical royal burgh wedge shape, and narrow burgage plots in
parallel lines, with the usual crop of mills, tanneries and distilleries
hugging the river.

population of 4,000 was set for the 1:500 scale, which became the standard for large mapping after 1863. Surveys at the ten feet scale were mainly financed by town councils who found the five feet scale insufficient for underground engineering operations. All the large-scale plans ceased publication after 1894 (municipally financed revisions apart) and there were no new large-scale plans until the 50 inch (1:1250) series (for major towns only) of World War Two. Maps at this scale had been produced for a few areas from 1911, but these were not original surveys, being photographic enlargements of 25 inch maps.

The 25 inch has remained the mainstay of Scottish mapping, being the largest scale at which many of the smaller burghs have ever been surveyed. The whole edition was revised before the First World War as part of a twenty year revision programme. The second revision (or third edition) was begun in 1904 but never completed. Thereafter it was decided that urban areas only should be revised on the twenty year cycle, a decision that was rescinded in 1928 in favour of a programme of continuous revision of rapidly changing areas.

The typology of towns

Some of the most useful insights into a town arise from comparison with other towns of similar background – both the similarities and the differences are instructive. Typologies can be constructed on various bases – the geographical situation, the administrative and legal history, or the main economic functions. Some functions are common to all present day towns. Tivy (1961) suggests that 'they all provide certain commercial, professional, social and public services . . . they all possess some industry; they all provide recreational facilities, and they are, of course, all places where people reside either permanently or temporarily'. Nevertheless, one main function is usually the moving force in a town's growth at any one time, and needs to be identified if a researcher is to make much sense of what is going on.

The oldest category is the fortress town, the direct descendant of the hilltop forts of the Iron Age. Edinburgh and Stirling, perched on their rocks, are the most obvious examples. Lynch (1988) finds 'the gentle rounded hills of a non-defensible nature' as at Lanark, Selkirk and Dunfermline more problematic. The military town was still a functional reality in the eighteenth century, with foundations such as Fort Augustus, and is still significant today, albeit with an international orientation, in the case of NATO bases.

To the pre-urban military nucleus was attached, in most cases, a medieval market town below the castle gate. It is generally agreed that the organization of an agricultural surplus is fundamental to the origin and existence of such towns. Very deliberate town-planning accounts for their structural similarities – the central market area with burgage plots at right-angles and the wide, straight or wedge-shaped main street; or (alternatively) the two parallel streets system (seen in Perth and other eastern seaboard towns). These were the traditional royal burghs, distinguished from lesser market centres known as burghs of barony, which were not self-governing beyond committees of feuars or bailies appointed by the superior. It was however the latter type of burgh which showed explosive growth in the economic expansion of the seventeenth century, with 64 foundations between 1600 and 1650.

Modern market towns are still surprisingly numerous, though the emphasis has now been reversed. Rather than serving as a processing centre for the agricultural produce of the surrounding countryside, they now act as a distribution centre for products made elsewhere (even from the far ends of the earth). One outstanding feature of such towns is that the number of services they provide is large and disproportionate to their size, because of their wide hinterland. Tivy (1961) notes that if such service centres lacked a local bus company, as did Biggar, their significance was much reduced.

The burghs of barony of the seventeenth century and later, and the numerous police burghs of the nineteenth century (many towns are both) have certain features which distinguish them readily from the older burghs. Even if the former are planned, their structure is less formal, with a relaxed use of space in layout, and less intense building in the centre. The smaller burghs may even have a few villas or semi-detached houses in the main street. The area behind the main street will be revealing, for the back rows, if they exist at all, will be much closer to the main street. Right-angle building out along burgage plots will also be less likely.

The regional centre is an extension of the local service centre. Tivy (1961) found that Dingwall's two newspapers, and the headquarters' buildings for administrative and marketing bodies whose sphere of influence extended well beyond the county boundary, qualified it as a minor regional centre. The largest centres of this kind are cities such as Aberdeen – one of the largest in the world at its latitude.

The industrial town first appeared in the seventeenth century, often as a burgh of barony such as the one-landlord towns of Alloa and Cockenzie. It was prevalent around the Firth of Forth, exploiting a cluster of advantages – access to North Sea trade (then as central to world trade as the Gulf is today), rich fishing, coal and salt-panning. Dramatic growth was reserved for the start of the nineteenth century, when Scotland's centre of gravity moved west. Swift response to new technologies led to astonishing growth rates, most explosively in Clydebank, which expanded from 3,000 people in 1881 to 43,000 by 1913.

Holiday and health resorts date from the eighteenth century, and flourished in counterpoint to the industrial towns. The *Dictionary of Daily Wants* 1859 contrasted the air of cities 'vitiated by the different processes of respiration, combustion and putrefaction' with sea air, known to be 'beneficial and invigorating' because of 'its constant agitation by the winds and tides'. Specific types of air (dry and bracing, soft and humid) were recommended for different complaints, so both inland and seaside resorts prospered. A thriving modern holiday town such as Pitlochry can be distinguished from a straightforward service centre by its high incidence of hotels, restaurants, souvenir and clothing shops. Millman (1975) talks of the 'rather pretentious, distinctively Scots, style of domestic Victorian architecture' of holiday towns. Interestingly, Pitlochry began life as a commercial centre.

An unexpected type of burgh was the suburban police burgh of the large cities, where middle class residents sought to maintain their exclusivity by taking advantage of the police acts of 1850 and 1862. It would be interesting to study whether their structure resembled that of an independent settlement or whether they were in fact suburbs in all but name. Glasgow reabsorbed the last of her satellites in 1912. Towns such as Leith, absorbed by Edinburgh in 1920, were ancient independent settlements which were sucked into suburban status through urban growth. The newest variant reflecting the symbiosis of town and hinterland is the residential dormitory town, seen particularly on the fringes of the central belt. The handful of new towns are another recent addition to Scottish typology.

Chapter Two

THE STORY OF A HOUSE

The houses we live in, however modern, are part of the historic fabric of towns, every bit as much as are great public buildings and monuments. The closeness of history to our homes is conveyed by the Scottish novelist Candia McWilliam in *A Case of Knives*: the passage captures the intangible and exciting relationship between objects and the passing of time.

> It is not a personal gift to me, but by accident it is mine. It has settled on me because I live in the house where it is living. . . . It is a fit sense of one's own unimportance and a dignity which is not of fabric or of history, but held up by the soothing knowledge of temporariness. . . . It is like custodianship, or a vocation. . . . I might walk out into a different century, but there the house would be, sheltering lives, indifferent to whose they were.

The historical imagination has its source in the contemplation of this relationship between change and permanence. In our towns we feel it closely; and in our homes in the most intimate way. The history of houses is both literally and metaphorically the bricks and mortar of urban studies, as any definition of a town must centre on a grouping of permanent human habitations.

Title deeds

Each owner-occupied property has attached to it a group of documents establishing a sound title. If you are a home owner, some or all of these deeds may be in your possession; equally they may be held by a solicitor or building society, but copies can usually be obtained. Title deeds are the easiest and most sensible starting point in the investigation of the history of a house. Difficulties of interpretation derive mainly from the fact that the Scots legal system has evolved through the adaptation and manipulation of more ancient principles designed for other purposes. However, it is not often necessary for the layman to understand in detail the technicalities of the resulting language or even the theoretical principles which underpin it. After all, conveyancing is concerned with some very basic and obvious transactions – buying, selling, inheriting or mortgaging. The understanding of the precise meaning of some simple key words in relation to these transactions will allow a confident interpretation of a document to be made.

The most important of the deeds relating to title is the *feu charter* or *feu disposition* – for most purposes the terms are synonymous. A humble home's charter has exactly the same significance as the great medieval charters adorned with seals that we see in museums. This does not mean that our houses date back to the middle ages. Very, very few of Scotland's properties survive from before the seventeenth century; indeed, only 0.7 per cent of its housing stock was built before 1851. Figures given by Adams (1978) also show very small numbers of nineteenth-century houses, 4.2 per cent of the stock dating from 1851–70 and 11 per cent from 1871–81. 18.3 per cent of houses date from 1891–1918, and two thirds of the total from since 1919. Of the minuscule pre-1851 figure, only a tiny proportion represents houses built before the mid-eighteenth century, when stone building became prevalent. The charter therefore does not signify an ancient stock of property. Rather, it indicates that the very real feudal system of the middle ages has been reinterpreted by generations of Scots lawyers to create a theoretical (and in a sense fictional) feudalism which is the foundation of modern conveyancing practice.

The essential idea of feudalism was that all land ultimately belonged to the crown (the superior), who granted or *feued* parts of it to vassals or *feuars* in return for services (such as produce or army service). Vassals in their turn could sub-feu to others, and thus were themselves both vassals and superiors. A key later development was the commutation of the medieval idea of service to the superior in favour of a down-payment (a *grassum*, which we would consider the sale price) together with an annual cash payment, in the form of feu duty, only recently abolished. It is interesting however that the ingrained principle of grant and service meant that Scots law could not easily accommodate the simple (to us) concept of anyone selling an existing feu, so that fictional contortions had to be resorted to for property to change hands, as will be explained below.

The modern feu charter bears some of the scars of these and

other tribulations. As in the middle ages, it will take the form of a grant from a named superior to a named vassal of a newly created estate, carved out of the larger estate which had in turn been granted to him. A vitally important point is that it is an estate which is feued, not a building. This is as true for a fourth-floor tenement flat as for a mansion house with policies. If a tenement building is burnt to the ground, each proprietor still owns the theoretical piece of sky where his or her apartment was situated. Not a single one of the legal documents referred to in the following pages will describe, except in the most general of formulae ('the villa known as such and such'), any of the buildings which stand upon the land, though they will describe the boundaries of the property in some detail. One consequence is that none of the documents will tell you when your house was built. In the case of properties constructed in the last 100 years or so, the feu charter may often stipulate that a house *is* to be built on the land and what it is to be built of, and how high and so on. Such strict controls were often laid down by the superior, for until recently his powers over planning and building control were very real. In the case of older property, the granting of a feu charter usually signifies that an existing house or group of houses which were part of a landed estate are for the first time being sold off from that estate, with no indication given whether they are two or 200 years old, or indeed whether they even exist. When it is further realized that the large estate was the norm in Scotland (68 men owned nearly half of Scotland in 1868) and that the vast majority of houses now in towns occupy land that was rural estates only a century or so ago, the difficulty of dating older houses other than through architectural style can be better appreciated. The recent government policy of council house selling is producing a current-day spate of feu charters similarly deficient in information about the age of the properties concerned, though in their case, ordnance survey maps and local government records will allow construction dates to be found.

The present-day tiny parcels of land which most home owners possess have sometimes resulted from a direct frag-mentation of a large estate, but more often the process has been progressive. A landowner for example might grant a feu to a builder or developer of a few acres; houses are then built and subsequently sold off as individual feus. In these cases, the feu charters for each stage in the process are identified in each individual title, for one can obviously have no claim on a property if one's superior does not possess a sound title to sell to you. Ideally, the title to each link in the chain should lead back to a feudal estate granted direct from the crown; and armed with this important name, the home owner can find out about any surviving estate papers which can throw light on the history of an older house or about the topography and use of the area before the house was built. If an estate was entailed (see page 48), the chances of finding specific information about a property are much increased.

One or two potentially puzzling clauses and expressions in feu charters or feu dispositions can be briefly explained. The *tenendas* clause names the superior of whom the lands are to be held and to whom, until recently, the feu duty usually had to be paid (though superiority could be bought and sold independently of the land itself). The *reddendo* is the annual feu duty payable. The *assignation of writs* is a promise by the grantor to make available or assign to the grantee all legal documents relevant to the defence of his or her title. Similarly *assignation of rents* conveys to the grantee any rents payable for the property purchased. The *obligation of relief* relieves the grantee of any debts or payments due on the estate prior to his or her entry. *Casualties* are obligations or payments imposed on the buyer; *burdens* are encumbrances on the property, most commonly the *standard security* or 'mortgage' for the money borrowed for the purchase. The *warrandice* clause insures the grantee against any fault in the grantor's authority to grant title, whether through error or malpractice. The clauses requiring registration will be discussed below.

A feu charter and feu disposition are granted only at the time of the creation of the estate. In most cases, there is a second vital element in a title – the evidence that the current property owner has acquired the estate. For if one is not the original grantee, one's name will not appear anywhere on the feu charter. The document which establishes the purchase, and which the seller is obliged to draw up, is called a disposition (the related verb is to dispone) which follows on from the initial missives of sale traded between the buyer's and seller's solicitors. The disposition contains several clauses similar in form to those in feu charters and feu dispositions.

There are other legal documents relating to a property, but the two so far discussed are key ones and the ones most likely to be in the house-holder's possession. For even if he or she is not the original recipient of the feu, that charter will have been copied for the solicitor in the investigation of the title and the solicitor will often pass the copy to the buyer. It will be useful, therefore, to recapitulate briefly on what they tell us and do not tell us about a house's history. They inform us about the owner of the land and buildings at the time the separate estate was created, and often the owner of the still larger estate when that was separated. They will tell us the first owner of the property and how much was paid for it. They will give very specific details about boundary fences and possibly adjacent properties and roads which existed at the time, together with their proprietors. It might be possible to deduce roughly when the house was built, and details of the materials to be used in construction, including even the quarry from which the stone was to be supplied, might be forthcoming. Information which cannot be learned include the exact date of construction (in some cases no date of any kind) or details of the owners intervening between the original disponee and the person who sold the property to you.

Sasine and registration

The title deeds discussed above are in themselves not worth the paper they are written on. It was always recognized that in addition some form of public display was an essential factor. The display that evolved was the ceremony of *sasine* (from the same root as the verb 'seize' – spelled *seise* in Scots legal terminology). In the ceremony, at which the feuar took possession, the superior and later his agent or bailie symbolic-ally handed over to the new vassal earth and stone from the site in question; in the burghs, a hasp and staple (the clasp and hoop to which a padlock was attached for fastening a door) were substituted. Without this ceremony, the *infeftment*, or putting into possession, was not complete. Its public nature 'performed publicly, with considerable ostentation and neces-sarily in daylight' (Monteath, 1958) had the intended effect of imprinting the proceedings on the memory of those con-cerned and their neighbours, so that in the event of future dispute (or more often a claim for inheritance) the courts could invoke this collective remembrance – obviously a somewhat unreliable procedure. One could of course also brandish one's charters, but the incidence of forgery was quite notorious.

In the late middle ages, a better solution was found in the

employment of an independent party to 'note down' the proceedings of sasine and infeftment – hence the name *notary public*. The notaries at this time were usually clerics and licensed by the crown. These masters of the scarce technology of writing and pioneers of the legal profession bore witness and recorded in their notarial writs many other transactions in ledgers known as *protocol books*. A notary was particularly welcome in burghs, for there alone were property holdings of a diversity and number which we take for granted today. Hence many notaries were closely associated with town councils, developing a semi-official status. An act of parliament in 1567 required that the books of deceased notaries should be sent to the provost and bailies for safe keeping. Later acts ordained that they should be transmitted to the king's clerk register, though many were not. As a result they survive both in old burgh records and in a Scottish Record Office collection. A good number of transcriptions have been published by the Scottish Record Society.

The final piece of the jigsaw in the evolution of modern sasine registration occurred at the beginning of the seventeenth century. The value of protocol books in countering fraud and clarifying property ownership led the government to introduce compulsory registers for the registration of sasine, such that no title was valid unless it had been recorded. The 1617 act explained the objective as one of eliminating 'the great hurt sustained by his Majesties Lieges, by the fraudulent dealing of parties, who haveing annaliet thair Landis, and received great summes of money therefore, yet, by their unjust concealing of some privat right formerly made by them, render the subsequent alienation done for great summes of money, altogether unproffitable' (in this paraphrase, the word 'alienation' is the equivalent of our word 'sale'). Since the time of the 1617 act, registers have been continuously kept; only in the last few years has a start been made to replace them with a new land registration system.

To have nearly 400 years of a continuous record of property transactions is an exceptional bounty enjoyed by Scottish local historians, and one which could be used far more than it is, particularly given the extent to which these records have been published. Entry initially was duplicated, appearing in a national (or *general*) register and a county based (or *particular*) register. The latter were abolished in 1868, since which time the general register has been organized on a county basis. The burghs, with their strong tradition of protocol books, were completely excluded from this system until their own Sasine Act of 1681, which noted the 'great security that the Kingdom enjoys by the publick Register of Seisings'. The act introduced independent burgh registers of sasines for each burgh, which were maintained into the twentieth century, being phased out between the mid-1920s and the 1960s following an act of 1926. The long independence of burgh registers is partly due to the burghs' unique form of feudal tenure, known as *burgage*. Unlike the general and particular registers, burgh sasine registers have not been published, but the lack is not as severe as it might appear, for by burgh is meant only those areas confined within the municipal boundaries, outside of which much of the suburban development of the towns we know today took place.

The Scottish Record Office has published seventeenth-century name indexes by sheriffdom, but the most important printed source is the abridged registers produced since 1821, arranged by county, in chronological order of entry. The series was extended backwards to cover the years from 1781. As noted above, the particular registers on which the abridgements were based were discontinued in 1868, so subsequent volumes, which became annual from that year, were drawn from the central register. Another innovation of 1868 was a full annual index of people and places. Some locally compiled indexes (not published) cover the years 1780–1868, and full card indexes to all sasines from the eighteenth century are maintained in the Scottish Record Office together with the full registers. Just as the registers had become a necessity, following the growth in land transactions with the disposal of church lands to the aristocracy after the Reformation, so the indexes became vital with the increasing scale of eighteenth-century economic activity. Indeed, one of the great values of the abridged registers is that they coincide with the development of a modern economy in which property is exploited as an investment and capital asset. A modern town has been referred to as a concrete expression of the relative monetary values of space.

Researchers outside Edinburgh will need to depend on access to sets of printed abridgements, which unfortunately were produced only in small numbers. Abridgements however do give all the information which most local historians would require. The student able to use the Scottish Record

Office will be able to draw on the resources of the Legal Search Room, still today the hub of research into sound title for all property transactions. The historian can have the records brought to the Historical Search Room, and is exempt from the fees charged to legal researchers. As well as abridgements for the whole country, the Legal Search Room holds the *Minute Books* which contain the full copies of the deeds and the *Presentment Books* which establish the strict chronological sequence of the entries. For the historian of a particular property, the most useful records are the *Reference Volumes*, in which copies of all the extracts are entered under person and place, providing instant access to all transactions since the mid-1870s relating to any property, including the divisions and sub-divisions of estates discussed above. Incidentally, the practicality of this reference system has led to its being adopted as the principle behind the new land title register which is currently supplanting sasine registration, the latter having always involved exhausting searches through past records to establish sound title.

Before 1858, most entries in the sasine register record an individual or body seising or taking possession of lands or superiority. Most common perhaps is the receiving of a feu from a superior under a feu charter or feu disposition, but there are many other significant categories.

It was suggested above that the concept of a sale of property conflicted with the original feudal idea of grant in return for service. Thomas Craig, the sixteenth-century jurist, looked with favour on the system, in which feus could not 'be acquired for money, but only "for honour and by favour of the lord", But in these desperate days purchase is the usual mode of acquiring them' (Craig, 1934). Straightforward resales or dispositions continued for a long time to masquerade as something else. One device that was frequently exploited was the right of a creditor to seize an estate – the prospective buyer took the fictional mantle of a creditor. Increasingly fictional too was the central role of the superior in the sale. For theoretically a vassal had no right to dispose of his gift, merely to return it whence it had come – his superior – who then in turn could dispose of it to another in a new charter. The charter granted to the new feuar could be of two types (largely indistinguishable in effect) – charters of *confirmation* and charters of *resignation ad favorem* . . . ('resignation in favour of' followed by the name of the new vassal). After 1858 *writs* of confirmation and resignation amount to much the same. The odd expression sometimes found in charters of resignation '*a me vel de me*' ('to me or from me') is a legal expedient to speed up the process of sale by fudging the relationship of superiority between the seller and his superior on the one hand and the purchaser on the other. A charter of *resignation ad remantiam* is slightly different – it records a genuine relinquishment of a feu to a superior (in our terms equivalent to selling the estate back into the larger estate from which it was detached). Charters of *novodamus* constitute a change in the terms or conditions of an existing feu charter.

In all these cases of 'sale', it is the new title holder who records the sasine on his own behalf through a notary, a situation which continued until 1868 (from 1858 the title holder could record 'a disposition to himself' instead of sasine). From 1848 the actual transfer of earth and stone by the superior or his bailie had become unnecessary, the symbolic idea of sasine being found sufficient. The prospect of submitting themselves to an endless round of such ceremonial could not have been pleasing to the commercially oriented landowners of burgeoning industrial towns. Instead, the operation was conducted in the notary's office, in association with some new legal forms which made their way into sasine registers. Previously, a *precept of sasine* (included with the charter from 1672) gave authority to the superior's representative to allow registration to be made, through a legal document called an *instrument of sasine*. An instrument in legal parlance is any document creating or confirming a right, or recording a fact.

Under the same commercial impetus, the major change of 1868, to which allusion has already been made, took place – the two separate processes of the sale (disposition) and the recording of the sale (sasine) were telescoped into one. Henceforth, dispositions themselves were recorded in the registers, without the need of a separate instrument. The latter became necessary only in a limited number of cases, for example when a single conveyance covered a number of properties. In such cases the general term *notarial instrument* supplants the more specific instrument of sasine. The most important difference for the local historian to bear in mind is that in the later registers, the seller's name appears first in straightforward dispositions, whereas previously the buyer's name had occurred first as the party seising the estate.

The fiction of the paternal involvement of the superior

extended even to the inheritance of a property, the deceased's heir having to seek entry as a vassal. The superior lost any real right to refuse in 1747, but the legal form remained. The simplest transaction was for the superior to issue a *precept of clare constat* (in Latin literally 'it has been made clear') or *precept of chancery* in the case of lands held direct from the crown. The heir recorded the precept in the register of sasines. *Writs of clare constat* are the post-1858 equivalents. The heir had two methods of establishing his right of succession, known as *general* and *special service*. Both forms appear in various guises through the history of sasines – charters of *resignation general service* (G.S. in the abridged registers) in the older volumes, then more recently notarial instruments declaring *right by general disposition and settlement*, and *extract decrees* of general or special service. The variety of forms really need not detain the local historian who is interested only in the fact of inheritance.

It was suggested above that one advantage of the published abridgements of sasine as historical evidence is that their inception coincided with the diffusion of the use of credit, the tensions between the suppliers and beneficiaries of credit being reflected in the ways a town developed. Mortgages (not a word often used in Scots legal language) and building societies are of relatively recent origin, for usury, or the loan of money at interest, was long regarded as contrary to ethical principles. Devices were of course resorted to, for example the purchase of the rent as a clandestine form of interest (infeftment for annual rent). A mortgage has one of two objectives: either to raise collateral on a property already owned, or to acquire funds to buy a property. The former is represented by the traditional Scots practice of *wadset*, in which the creditor took over the management of an estate.

A more modern idea is to raise a loan through a bond, which honestly acknowledges that one function of money is to make money. Of course the bondholder must acquire rights over the property as security. Property on land in Scots law is known as heritable property, hence the term *heritable bond*, which is basically a combination of wadset and annual rent. The right over the property held by the bondholder was naturally also recorded in the sasine register to protect his or her interest and to prevent the debtor selling the estate to an unsuspecting buyer whilst it was still burdened. Hence were recorded *bonds in disposition and security*. Originally, an instrument of sasine was necessary, but from the mid-nineteenth century, power was given for the direct recording of a bond, just as a few years later, direct recording of dispositions was made possible. The modern bond is the Scots standard security – the equivalent of the English mortgage. Provision was made for the inheritance of bonds just as for any other property, the debtor making a *writ of acknowledgement* (acknowledging that the heir was the new creditor). A more sophisticated financial world also demanded a creditor's right to transfer his bond to a third party, dealing in bonds as one would in shares, by means of an *assignation*, similarly recorded in the register. A defaulting debtor would find his property being attached by his creditor, who establishes his title by the process of *adjudication*, also duly recorded in the register. The creditor could not immediately dispose of the estate – the debtor had ten years in which to redeem the debt before foreclosure.

Once the bond had been paid off (periods of 15 years were usual in the nineteenth century) the creditor's interest of course lapsed, and an entry in sasine was necessary to cancel the disposition in security, by means of a *renunciation* or *discharge*, granted by the creditor.

Today the majority of loans are given by building societies, local authorities and banks, but this was not the case in the nineteenth century. Banks in fact were notable for their absence from the housing market. Building societies originated as self-help organizations, known as *benefit building societies*. The two earliest Scottish examples were both in Kirkcudbright (founded 1808 and 1810). These societies were cooperative enterprises for the building of houses (112 erected in the Kirkcudbright case). Members of the cooperative often held lotteries or auctioned their funds to choose who was to get houses first. Different in style were the later *permanent* building societies, whose basic function was to loan money on behalf of investors. The latter were mainly English, and have penetrated into Scotland fairly recently.

Money for loans was more commonly accumulated from a variety of sources, and put together by accountants and, particularly, lawyers, often in association with house factors. The sources included trust funds from charities, marriage settlements and bequests, as well as the individual savings of numerous members of the lower middle classes, to provide, in the words of Elliott and McCrone, (1980) 'investment income, occasional speculative gains, security against old age, widowhood and spinsterdom'. The safety of the investment was expressed to the Hunter Committee in the words 'stone and lime . . . something we can go and see'. Indeed, many bondholders bankrupted builders and landlords by calling in their bonds (which normally yielded 4½ to 5 per cent interest) during times of recession. These 'little bundles of capital' were further augmented by funds from another kind of building society, which approximated to an investment association, with subscription shares for loans to builders and speculators as well as householders. Their names appear in connection with a large number of bonds recorded in sasine registers – for example the Western Provident and Building Society, the Scottish Prudential Investment Association, the Standard Property Investment Company and the North British Property Investment Company.

The prevalence of bonds (Adams (1978) records a 1930s estimate from the Scottish Office research papers of 85 per cent of properties being subject to them) is reflected by a large number of sasine entries for any one property. The process in fact usually began with a middleman – a speculator or builder – who would initially feu the whole site from a landowner with finance from bonds. He in turn would issue feu charters of smaller blocks to partnerships, builders and consortia of businessmen or tradesmen, who would set about building the houses, again financed by bonds. The small scale of most of these developments has been illustrated by Elliott and McCrone (1980) who used the example of the tenements in Caledonian Crescent, Edinburgh, in which every one of the first 15 plots was financed by a different builder. According to Rodger (1975), between 1873 and 1914 in the cities of Aberdeen, Dundee and Edinburgh, nearly 40 per cent of all building approvals granted by the Dean of Guild courts were for one house only. In 30 of the next largest burghs, the figure was nearer 54 per cent. Once a tenement or house was completed, a buyer would be found, raising yet another set of loans. The buyer was nearly always a landlord (often a tradesman, spinster or widow of small means) who rented the property in whole or in part to tenants. Owner occupation was not widespread before the First World War, even among the upper middle classes. Another source of investment came from the ground annual, an annual payment similar to feu duty which originated as a device to circumvent feu charters which prohibited sub-feuing. Tenement builders in particular achieved thereby a permanent source of annual income.

From the above description, it will be clear that the study of property ownership and finance through deeds and sasines can open a window on both the social history and the geographic and economic development of towns. Though such studies have been undertaken by professional historians in the major cities, not much has been done in the numerous small towns. There is thus a great opportunity for the amateur local historian to make an important contribution, with the added interest of dealing with the speculations and property owner- ship of local families possibly still known in the area, even of the researcher's own family.

Valuation rolls

Valuation rolls are a well-known source which can be used in the same context. Each entry (the organization is by street) details the name and number of the property, the owner, the tenant, the occupier and the rateable value. Up to the mid- 1950s, there is an added bonus, in that the occupations of tenants and occupiers are also included.

The origin of rating is complex, as is that of local taxation in general. In the traditional pre-nineteenth-century burghs, town councils raised most of what they required through the leasing out of customs, market and harbour dues, and multure (milling charges). These monies formed part of what was known as the common good, which was sufficient for most needs, even being used as collateral for raising loans, which were repaid from the same source. Cleansing costs were often covered by the sale of manure; policing was the responsibility of the citizens 'watching and warding'; small amounts were raised by indirect taxation (especially on ale and beer) under local acts of parliament.

This mixed bag persisted in burghs up to the end of the nineteenth century. Indeed it was not until 1870 that councils were given powers to abandon them and substitute a rate. Despite this, only 24 were levying a rate by 1900. Sources of common good income 'have taken such a long time to die' noted the historian of Scottish local finance (Turner, 1908) 'because the burghal inhabitants persisted in viewing them as taxes falling mainly on their rural neighbours . . .' – it was the latter for example who paid market dues when bringing their produce to town.

The origins of valuation rolls are therefore to be sought not in local burghal taxation, but from two other sources. Firstly, there was national taxation, to which burghs were traditionally expected to contribute one-sixth. The method of collection was left vague and originally varied from burgh to burgh. The national taxation became annual from the seventeenth century, and was known as the cess or land tax; burghs continued to contribute corporately up to 1896. By that time the one-sixth was usually paid through a rate upon inhabitants (the technical definition of a rate is that the sum needing to be collected is predetermined, and apportioned accordingly among those liable).

The second formative influence in the development of valuation rolls was levies, made both inside and outside of burghs to support functions partly or entirely outwith the responsibility of town councils, such as poor relief, schooling, roads and (increasingly in the nineteenth century) public health measures. Methods of allocation were various and with numerous variants, including a levy on property on the basis of rental, on inhabitants according to their means, on owners and occupiers, or any mixture of all the above.

Before the mid-nineteenth century therefore, each locality will have produced a very individual collection of property registers, or even no property registers at all. Linlithgow, exceptionally, between 1679 and 1695 produced seven listings of inhabitants, plus a permanent roll of all householders and a roll of house proprietors which, together with the rolls of the national hearth tax levied in 1691, 'allows a virtual house-by-house reconstruction of the town to be made . . .' (Flinn, 1977).

In the first half of the nineteenth century, a series of acts such as the police acts (the first being 1833) became the basis of important new rates, and led to the regularization of assessment through the 1854 Valuation Act. This act is therefore an important landmark for the study of property, for it provided for systematic valuation, annually amended, on a uniform basis throughout the country. One can be fairly confident that every habitable property existing at, or built since that time, has been recorded, with all the information outlined at the beginning of this section. The history of the occupation of your home can be traced from year to year, supplemented for most of the nineteenth century (1841–91) by the decennial census enumeration books which, though primarily intended as an enumeration of the population, paid a lot of attention to housing (particularly the number of rooms) and listed (by property) all the inhabitants, including children and servants, their ages, occupations and places of birth.

Dean of guild records

Many dean of guild courts were an emergency response to nineteenth-century housing conditions. The courts did have an ancient provenance, originating as sub-committees of the general court of the guild in the medieval royal burghs; but the powers of the dean of guild had been progressively attenuated through the jealous opposition of town councils, the process of erosion reaching its furthest development in the Municipal Corporations (Scotland) Act 1833. The dramatic reversal in the fortunes of the institution came with the Burgh Police (Scotland) Act 1862 which allowed all town councils and police commissioners, including the large number recently established, to set up such courts or their equivalents. Twenty had taken advantage of the legislation by 1880, and 189 by 1912 (by which time they had become compulsory under the 1892 Burgh Police (Scotland) Act).

The dean of guild courts insisted that all proposed building in towns be subject to scrutiny, following the nineteenth-century environmental priorities of public health, water, drainage and lighting rather than the architectural and amenity considerations of present-day planning departments. However, it has been stated that the powers of these distinctively Scottish courts as 'scrutineers of external structural standards' exceeded those of their English counterparts, and that 'the rigours with which [they] . . . discharged this function prompted anguished cries for relaxation towards the end of the century as informed observers commented on how unduly demanding building regulations unnecessarily increased building costs . . .' (Rodger, 1983). Builders were sometimes accused of attempting to evade dean of guild regulations by building ouside burgh boundaries. Robert McAlpine for instance constructed the 'Holy City' for the Singer factory just outside Clydebank's boundaries. He countered claims about poor materials and techniques by pointing out that the rent of £9 charged to tenants was £2 10s less than the average in Clydebank. Be that as it may, the benefit for the historian of

houses of the series of Dean of Guild *Approved Duplicate Plans*
and associated minute books is considerable.

Entail

Many of today's suburban estates developed outwith the
jurisdiction of burghs. For the older of these houses one source
of information of comparable quality to the dean of guild
records is the *Registers of Improvements on Entailed Estates*
maintained by the sheriff courts from 1770 to the late
nineteenth century. An entailed or tailzied estate was defined
by the jurist Thomas Craig as 'a feu which transmits to a
definite series of substitute heirs in an oblique line according to
an artificial distinction, whereby the true line of legal succession is cut away and disregarded'. Tailzie means cutting –
from the same root as tailor. The most important legislation
was the 1685 Act Concerning Tailzies, passed at a time when
many aristocratic families feared a diminution of their power.
They were concerned to ensure the preservation of their
estates intact, avoiding the fragmentation that could occur in
the absence of a male heir.

One of the consequences of entail was a prohibition against
raising loans against improvements on the estate, a state of
affairs which roused the indignation of Adam Smith and other
observers in the age of agricultural improvements. Adam
Smith estimated that one third of Scotland's land was entailed
in the second half of the nineteenth century; some nineteenth-
century calculations claimed up to one half.

Measures to counter entail's stultification of modern estate
management began with the 1770 Act to Encourage the
Improvement of Lands Held under Settlements of Strict
Entail, and provided for the 'building of villages and houses'
on such estates, on condition that the proprietor specified the
kind of improvement intended, sending a written copy or
plans to the heir of entail and duplicates to the sheriff court. He
was also obliged to lodge with the sheriff annually 'an account
of the money expended by him in such improvements during
twelve months preceding . . . with the vouchers by which the
account is to be supported when payment shall be demanded
or sued for'.

The sheriff duly recorded these in a register. A plethora of
further acts followed in the nineteenth century, some to
facilitate the building of 'cottages for labourers, farm servants

and artisans', others encouraging the planting of public buildings such as schools and churches. Most sheriff court records are now lodged in the Scottish Record Office where they can be studied.

Chapter Three

HOMES AND SUBURBS

Being rude about suburbia is a favourite British pastime, but suburbia is where nearly all of us live. Lewis Mumford's caustic remark has already been recorded, but at the same time he praised the 'free use of space' oriented for sunlight, summer breezes and view, 'the precise opposite of most historic cities'. Conzen (1968) picks on the 'crescent's curves descended through the spas and watering-places of Regency England, and the quadrants of Nash's Regent Street, to the age of the close-packed . . . villa, and the semi-detached house, to which they have no relevance whatever. To call a loop of semi-detached houses a crescent is to make an emotional noise, not a statement'. The foolish pretentiousness of many suburbs is of course obvious, but perhaps not unendearing. Anita Brookner in her novel *Lewis Percy* (1989) finds some more positive qualities, in that 'to be suburban was almost a calling in itself, involving steadiness, a certain humility in the face of temptation, social or otherwise, and loving, almost painful attachment to home'.

The unique and eclectic contribution of suburbia to the history of domestic architecture has also been a cause of controversy, from the time of Ruskin's description of the houses as 'of rotten brick, with various iron devices to hold it together'. Naismith (1989) weighs in with an observation on the unspoilt nature of early nineteenth-century Scottish towns which 'had not yet begun to suffer from later ill-fitting additions as unbecoming as an off-the-peg duffle coat'. Barrett and Phillips (1987) suggest that 'it is perhaps . . . contentment and satisfaction with the compromise that is suburbia – a state that has been achieved without the help of architects or the diversions of town life – that has itself led to criticism. Suburbia's persistent refusal to fall down or decay has always been a source of irritation'.

Whatever the arguments, the local historian of towns cannot ignore suburbia without closing his or her eyes to the greater part of the subject, at least in terms of surface area. To take one example, Glasgow's area grew during the nineteenth century from 715 hectares to 5,134 hectares, and further boundary extensions in 1926 and 1938 doubled its size yet again, all of which growth was dominated by suburban domestic development.

The tenement

Noting that nearly 60 per cent of the Scottish population lived in state housing compared with 29 per cent in England, Adams (1978) commented that 'Scotland has always been a nation of tenants'. One of the important reasons for the difference has been the tradition of tenement life. The origin of the tenement in Scotland has been variously traced, to the feuing system (see below), to the need for heat conservation in a cold climate, and to the defensive capacities of tall buildings. The pends cut through from the High Streets of older burghs could be individually barred, making it necessary for an assailant to fight for each block in turn. It was also necessary for those who wished to benefit from burghal trading privileges to dwell within the town's gates, whose limits were fixed by the original charters. As the economies of the medieval burghs began to outstrip the burghs' capacity to absorb them, buildings were squeezed inside the walls on the original burgesses' agricultural plots, known as tofts. According to Mair (1988) over 75 per cent of the land was covered with infill building of this kind in seventeenth-century Ayr, Glasgow, Dumfries, Dundee, Arbroath, Stonehaven, Aberdeen, Inverness and Dunfermline, with accompanying pressure for upward expansion.

Not too much emphasis should be placed on this development, for, despite isolated examples such as the 'great tenement' of four storeys which stood in Glasgow's Trongate with a date stone of 1591, most tenements outside Edinburgh were of two storeys with an attic. Indeed, in most small burghs where land pressures remained less pronounced, the two-storey version with outside stair of wood or stone was described as being still the predominant form at the time of the Royal Commission on Housing in Scotland, reporting in 1916. Most of the examples then standing (and many remain today, despite the large-scale redevelopments of the 1930s and 1960s) dated from the first part of the nineteenth century, sometimes beginning life as single houses which were subsequently subdivided. The Royal Commission summary report

(1918) found they had 'ceilings low and requiring repair, walls very damp, no water in the house, and in many cases rooms dark and evil-smelling, no water-closet accommodation or very little, and that exceedingly bad'.

The nineteenth-century four-storey tenement, said to be approximately the height of the old Scottish baronial towers, is a fundamental part of the Scottish townscape, not only in the four great cities of Aberdeen, Dundee, Edinburgh and (overwhelmingly) Glasgow, but also in numerous industrial towns. In fact, there are small pockets in nearly every burgh, sometimes in a reduced three-storey version but sharing an obvious architectural parentage. One reason which has been given is the feuing system. Unlike the English leaseholding where a proprietor who sold land stood to benefit in the long run from the betterment of the property (come the day of his reversionary rights), feuing was a permanent alienation. Although there was a guaranteed regular income from feu duty, it was eroded by inflation. Furthermore, the right to exact it was shared in all the stages of subinfeudation – by builder, house factor and house purchaser – all of which increased the pressure to maximize the number of feu-duty payers. The economic case for high-rise was intensified by the relative shortage of capital, of which there was a net outflow from Scotland during the nineteenth century. Attractive investment with high returns became a necessity to stop the exit of funds. One question, however, which has not been satisfactorily answered is why, in the main, four-storey building was regarded as the maximum, even after steel-frame technology, as developed in the United States, made much higher structures possible.

The density of tenement building in Glasgow in the nineteenth century was phenomenal. The restrictive natural contours of the city can only explain in small part how, in 1914, 700,000 people were housed in an area of three square miles – the most heavily populated central area in Europe. Eighty-five per cent of her population, writes Checkland (1976) were 'born, raised, laboured and died in their world of tenements'.

The first generation of four-storey tenements was influenced by the pioneer factory housing of New Lanark as well as by traditional forms. This generation, photographed by Thomas Annan, was swept away by the City Improvement Trust in the late nineteenth century. When it is learned that

43,000 Irish emigrated to Glasgow between December 1848 and March 1849, one is not surprised that the quality of the housing provided was rudimentary. Later tenements, including those for the working classes, were more soundly constructed, and many blocks surviving today proclaim their construction date on embossed stone plaques high up on their walls. It has been claimed that most town dwellers rarely raise their eyes above two or three metres – local historians will miss much unless they behave otherwise. The quality of late nineteenth-century building – with costs 40 per cent higher than in England – was partly due to the use of expensive materials such as dressed stonework facing. These facings – 'polished ashlar frontages of white and red sandstone' Worsdall (1979) calls them – sometimes embellished with string courses of a different colour or with rustication of the stonework, give a solidity to Scottish towns which immediately identifies them. The scale, character and sandstone colouring of many town centres too is determined by the tenement; also suburban shopping streets, where the ground floor of working-class tenements is given over to retail use. The impression is reinforced by the ring of building around the inner city along the main traffic routes, as in Edinburgh.

The tenement has been as much a middle-class as a working-class residence – the gentility of the apartments above the scruffy shops of some small burghs can be a surprise. In Glasgow, Worsdall noted that even two-apartment flats sometimes had bell-pulls for servants. The best had three to four rooms, plus kitchen and bathroom, and boasted the new distinctive bow windows or oriels which took advantage of technological innovations in glass – a flood of sunlight moderated by the discretion of lace curtains. The finest Edinburgh examples, in the words of McWilliam (1975), display 'the large scale splendour that can speak from a distance, with artfully composed elevations and majestic corner towers, sometimes of baronial outline'. What is known as the 'baronial revival treatment' evolved in Edinburgh in the 1880s and was especially associated with model housing schemes such as Well's Court in Dean village and the east side of Glasgow's Saltmarket, 'its Scottishness almost apologetically announced by a few crow-stepped gables' suggests Frank Walker (1985). The west side of Saltmarket, built in the 1890s, was more pronouncedly Scots, and the style was still being used up to the First World War, as in Rothesay's Russell Street of 1910.

Glasgow had produced its own tradition of tenement architects, so by no means all tenements emanated from the pattern books of speculative builders. The one-man firm of George F. Boyd for instance produced 354 plans between 1886 and 1911. He was working in a tradition established by some of the greatest of Glasgow architects, notably Alexander 'Greek' Thomson, who built tenement terraces in a style which had evolved from the classical sweep of Georgian terraces as seen in Edinburgh's west end.

For all the grandeur of middle-class tenements, they shared with the working-class versions the maligned common stair, which W. T. Gairdner, Glasgow's first medical officer of health, described as 'a receptacle of foul air, usually closed at the top, and receiving the effluvia from all the houses on the stair . . .' Such censure led to the creation of the balcony tenement, of which pioneering examples were at Rosemount Buildings and Patriot Hall, Stockbridge, both in Edinburgh. The rationale of the balcony tenement is illustrated by the prospectus of the block built by the Glasgow Workman's Dwelling Company in 1892 which boasted of 'through ventilation from front to back of each house'. The iron balcony rails are a familiar feature on many tenements from this time forward, and still have a strong influence on the design of blocks of flats, with concrete now usually preferred to iron. Their story becomes linked with council house building after the First World War, for a chapter of Scotland's building history came to an end with Lloyd George's Finance Act of 1910, which signed the economic death warrant of private tenement construction.

Middle class suburbs

Suburbs outside the jurisdiction of town councils existed from the middle ages. Occasionally they were burghs in their own right, such as Newton upon Ayr and Portsburgh beside Edinburgh. Often on the other side of the river by which towns stood, they seem to have been in part oppressed and in part tolerated, for despite their regular infringement of burgh monopolies in manufacture and trading, they provided useful low-level services. Even in nineteenth-century towns, tanneries, breweries and the like are often found in these areas.

Technically the burghal monopolies survived until the Burgh Trading Act 1846 which made it 'lawful for any person to carry on or deal in merchandise, and to carry on or exercise any trade or handicraft, in any burgh or elsewhere in Scotland without being a burgess of such burghs, or a guild brother, or a member of any guild, craft or incorporation'. However, long before that time, the regulations had become a dead letter. Expansion outwith the town walls occurred from the eighteenth century, and that this was domestic suburban expansion has been obscured by the fact that most of the resulting mansion houses of wealthy merchants have now been converted to commercial use. Edinburgh, with its Georgian new town, was exceptional in that the new suburb was conceived on a grand scale and totally detached from the old town (partly because of the latter's difficult topography). Georgian terraces on the Edinburgh model are to be found (on a smaller scale) in many towns. Examples are Ancaster Square in Callander, Charles Abercrombie's neoclassical Golden Square, Silver Street and Lindsay Street in Aberdeen (on the reduced architectural scale of two storeys, with cornice, low parapet and slate roof, mainly refitted as offices in Edwardian times) and Dundee's dormer town of Broughty Ferry. Paisley's eighteenth-century expansion is explained by the names of its gridiron development of Lawn Street, Gauze Street, Silk Street and Cotton Street. Less pretentious developments of artisan and working class Georgian cottage housing also occurred, for example in the planned town of Keith (post-1750) and in Eaglesham.

The gridiron pattern was to have a long association with the town, in domestic terrace developments up to the mid-nineteenth century (usually typified by an absence of front garden), and thereafter more associated with commercial sector construction. The plain unpretentiousness of the one- or two-storey terrace town house in stone, with sash windows, dormers (sometimes) and slate roofs (or red tiles, along the east coast) can be found all over Scotland, and has continued to influence the scale and character of twentieth-century building at its best. The result, in the opinion of Naismith (1989), is the small town 'architectural variety shows to which everyone, apart from architectural purists, can wholeheartedly respond', and which can be contrasted with 'the grand opera of the planned frontages of some of the cities'.

The ethos of many Georgian terrace developments reflected

the snobbish desire to live in what appeared to be a palace, albeit only in a tiny section of it. One interesting and curious variant are the houses at the Colonies and elsewhere in Edinburgh, where separate entrances for top and bottom flats at back and front convey the illusion that each householder occupies a two-storey house. A linear successor of the Georgian terrace is the tenement block, which shares the philosophy of communal architecture in which individuality has no room for expression. Adams (1978) links the tradition to the low incidence of home ownership, adding that 'to the visitor, many Scottish towns appear uniform and dull, dominated as they are by council houses whose tenants seem to feel little responsibility for, or pride in the external appearance of their homes'.

A contrasting snobbery has also been at work over the last 150 years – that of aspiring to live in a miniature country house, with all the associated idiosyncracies popularly attributed to the British aristocracy and their homes. The individuality of the 'home as castle' is quite at odds with the gridiron philosophy of taming the contours of nature with straight lines – and incidentally those contours often make a nonsense of the geometry when crudely applied, as it was more often than not. For this competing philosophy, nature was to be welcomed, and its history is that of the attempted reconciliation of the rural and the urban.

Some of the more grandiose mansions built on the outskirts of towns in the eighteenth century were still town houses with street frontages and little privacy. The most extreme and incongruous example is Lauderdale House (1736), a country house which dominates one end of Dunbar High Street, with the disadvantage of permitting the local urchins to watch one eating dinner. The more discerning built their detached mansions in miniature parks in imitation of the policies of the country house. In Glasgow, for example, there were Shaw-field Mansion (built 1717 in three and a half acres of garden) and James McNayr's house on Woodland Hill, nicknamed 'McNayr's Folly' by his contemporaries who saw it 'as an out of the way place from which to pursue business in the city' (quoted by Dicks, 1985). The distance would be considered laughable by today's commuter.

From these pioneers the ethos of the country in the town has spread – partly in reaction to the disease and pollution that afflicted industrial settlements. It spawned the villa, set in its own private garden, and its poorer relative the semi-detached, and even led to the terrace with front gardens – a somewhat contradictory aesthetic (the gardens of Georgian terrace developments such as those in Edinburgh were communal, not private, and detached altogether from the houses themselves). Later came cheaper versions of absolute privacy – the bungalow, the inter-war council house and latterly the acres of Wimpeyland, all arranged in their groves, parks and avenues, even if there is no tree in sight. Pre-nineteenth-century towns knew only 'streets' and 'gates' (the latter an Anglo-Saxon version of 'street', nothing to do with gates). The Victorians made 'road' the prevalent form, and popularized all the rural connotations.

The nineteenth-century villa was the first substantial manifestation of the rural philosophy, and the suburb in which it sat was an integral part of the design. Dr Cleland, a Glasgow statistician, noted in 1837 that 'families, who were formerly content to live in a flat of a house in the old, have now handsome self-contained houses in the new parts of the town'. As Burnett (1978) explains: 'Once it had been shown by the sanitary enquiries of the 1840s how many diseases were spread by human filth, and once the statisticians had demonstrated how widely mortality rates varied in different areas of town and in different occupations, the poor became unacceptable as near neighbours'.

The middle-class colonizers of suburbs demanded specific qualities of their new environment which have been investigated by Simpson (1977). It had to be exclusive to the upper middle class ('the whole of these 450 acres are to be occupied solely by Dwelling-Houses of a superior description' runs the promotional literature for Kelvinside) and clauses to this effect were inserted in the feu charters and ground annuals. Prospective buyers also insisted on clear buffer zones between their estates and those of the working class and industrial areas. This segmentation of towns into district zones for different classes and different functions marks a departure from traditional practice and is one of the features which distinguishes the structure of a modern town from its predecessors. It serves as a reminder that villa development, despite its seeming randomness (a deliberate effect), was every bit as much planned as a Georgian square.

Another demand from potential suburbanites was for a healthy climate, including the all-important fresh air, dubbed

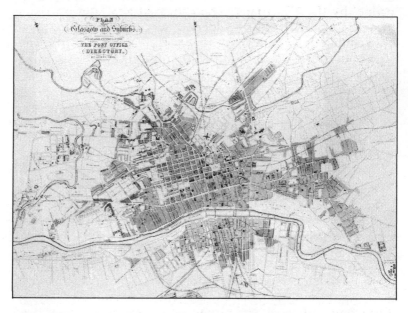

'Plan of Glasgow and Suburbs Engraved Expressly for the Post Office Directory' by Joseph Swan. Post Office and other local directories are valuable sources of commercial and public information, with maps such as this as a bonus. The plan shows early grid development in Hutchinsontown (once a prestige area) and glimmerings of the new suburban ideal with the tell-tale Woodside Terrace in Kelvingrove. The rise of the modern town is indicated by the proliferation of railway stations and the necropolis.

'ozone' by the Victorians. The choice of airy sites on rising ground (spurned by the builders of traditional towns which were huddled under the lee of any protecting feature) often marks out the Victorian suburb. The sea too was invested with curative powers, initially through being 'taken', like spa waters, subsequently through immersion and latterly, from the 1860s, for the properties of its bracing air. Consequently the Victorians built their 'marine villas' boldly facing out to the water, where their predecessors had built to turn sides and backs to the sea. A considerable number of seaside towns along the Clyde, Forth and Tay owe their existence and prosperity to the anxious quest for a salubrious climate. Such towns acted as dormitory suburbs as well as holiday resorts, for upper middle class families from the cities would rent villas for the season, with the paterfamilias remaining in town during the week at the family's urban residence.

Communication was of course another of the vital factors in the choice of suburban development sites. Initially, proximity to the centre of town was vital to accommodate the tradition of lunching at home. The blazing of such routes as the Great Western Road in Glasgow in 1841 to a distance of two miles, from the business district of St George's Cross to the western frontier at Anniesland Cross, promoted feuing half a mile deep on either side. The only transport then was a carriage, but for the succeeding generation horse trams (from 1870) and suburban railways greatly extended the range.

Suburban architecture

The architecture of the nineteenth-century suburb can be summed up in Maurice Lindsay's assessment (1987) that the 'Victorians may not have produced a new architectural style of their own, but they were wonderfully inventive in reinterpreting and creating variations upon the great styles of antiquity, shamelessly combining them when it suited their purpose'. The suburban tradition thus presents an interesting exercise for local historians in interpreting the elements in any particular mixture and tracing these often obscure symbols to their architectural homelands. As suggested earlier, part of the attraction of the suburb is its cosy and cavalier debasement of artistic ideals, in the name of individuality. The aesthetic of the Victorian villa and its twentieth-century descendants may be firmly placed within the 'picturesque' tradition, manifested in its early stages in the highly-prized eccentricity of the eighteenth-century folly.

The simple Georgian house styles lost their hundred-year-long popularity in the 1840s. Technological advances were a contributing factor, as they provided options not feasible before. Glass production for example, which was previously a craft industry, became concentrated in the hands of three firms – Pilkington, Chance and Hartley – the last named being responsible for the innovation of thin plate glass casting in 1847. This invention coincided with the reduction and final abolition in 1851 of a long-standing window tax. With further momentum from sanitary reformers, who equated lack of sunlight and ventilation with high levels of disease, it is little wonder that the traditional well-proportioned Georgian façade should give way to somewhat more luxuriant and immoderate forms.

In the resulting free-for-all, three main architectural influences fought for attention. Italianate models inspired both major features such as flat topped campaniles or bell towers (made even more popular by Prince Albert's championship at Osborne on the Isle of Wight) and details such as large overhanging eaves and horizontal string courses. Windows were often elegantly arched in Romanesque or Venetian style. The appearance of machine-made mouldings and castings made possible the reproduction of hand-carving styles which in their original form would have been prohibitively expensive for the middle classes. This freedom of reproduction, chosen at random from standard pattern books, was in many ways the enemy of good architecture.

Riotous moulding became even more prevalent with the Gothic style, encouraged by Ruskin's celebration of the organic, crudely interpreted in stylized curves. The term Gothic, say Barrett and Phillips (1987), 'as applied to Victorian architecture is almost indefinable, since it was used by the Victorians to cover any style that was not classical'. It prevailed from the 1860s, overtaking the Italian in popularity, though 'Swiss barge boards, Tudor chimneys and rustic porches might be added with cheerful obliviousness of any incongruity'. Gothic features include steep pitched roofs with mansards, turrets, pointed-arch windows and decoration with carved foliage.

The third major influence on building style was Scots Baronial, whose features were described by Robert Kerr in

The Gentleman's House of 1864 as 'small turrets on the angles of buildings, sometimes carried up from the ground, and sometimes built out on corbelling; crowstepped gables, battlemented parapets; small windows generally . . . and over the whole in one form or another a severe, heavy, crude, castellated character'. Modern judgements of the Baronial have been rather caustic. Naismith (1989) for example considers that it 'no more succeeded in producing an authentic Scottish building than could be produced by draping tartan over Salisbury cathedral'.

The popularity of Baronial was based on national enthusiasm, the castellations echoing with fantasies of celtic independence. 'From Charles Wilson's rather refined Scots villas in Dundee's West End (*c.*1851) to John Ednie's gnarled and quirky mansions at Whittinghame Drive, Glasgow (1910), suburban villas all across the country had proclaimed that a Scotsman's home too could be his castle' says Walker (1985). The Gothic and the Italianate were more subtle appeals to, respectively, quasi-religious and Renaissance ideals. 'There is sanctity in a good man's home' said John Ruskin, 'I say that if men lived like men indeed their houses would be temples – temples . . . in which it would make us holy to be permitted to live'.

Towards the end of the nineteenth century, a more genuinely contemporary aesthetic comes into vogue – that of the Arts and Crafts movement inspired by William Morris and his friends. However, the transfer of their handcraft-inspired ideals to the mass construction techniques of suburbia could not be achieved without considerable loss: the end result is sometimes nothing more than a wooden porch or balcony with mock Tudor timbering, leaded glass and un-Scottish brick. The homeliness of Arts and Crafts however continued to influence the scale of building and can still be seen in recent housing styles.

Subsequent architectural movements have tended to pass suburbia by. More profound revivals of vernacular tradition by the likes of Robert Lorimer, and the Art Nouveau of Charles Rennie Mackintosh, are superbly represented in mansions, but these buildings are untypical both in their size and their architectural originality. The later so-called International Style (the streamlined, flat-roofed look) suffered the same fate. Creations such as the flats of Ravelston Gardens in Edinburgh described by Charles McKean (1988) as 'like three enormous beached ocean liners' are much less common than the theft of decorative features such as the 'moderne' or 'suntrap' curved metal-framed windows designed to receive as much sunlight as possible. Such features were stuck onto conventional suburban façades.

Sunshine was also part of the philosophy behind the more substantial twentieth-century speculative building phenomenom of the bungalow. Built originally in seaside resorts, they reflected prevailing ideas of healthy living – sunshine, fresh air and, if not the sea, the countryside. At the turn of the century, such ideas were seen as liberating and faintly daring after the formality of Victorian social life, in the same way as the Pre-Raphaelite dress adopted by their bohemian inhabitants eschewed stiff and unnatural corseting of the body. The association of these images with the design of 1930s bungalows for the respectable middle class confirms the general observation of Jones (1968) that 'the persistence of vestigial forms as purely decorative features beyond their functional origin is a commonplace of experience. Indeed, such persistence is the very stuff of local history. . . . We often fail to read back from the decoration to the conditions which brought it into being. Hence we do not appreciate the nature of the human responses at the point of origin of the decoration'.

One particular feature that responded to the cluster of ideas behind the bungalow movement was the choice of a site on gently rising ground, with each bungalow itself often also provided with a landscaped hillock of its own. Hill sites, previously difficult for suburban development because of the limited draft power of horses and carts, became cheaply accessible with motor transport. The massed ranks of bungaloid growth in Edinburgh's Duddingston may be on rising ground; what we forget today, so much are they part of the urban fabric, is that they originated as an escape from the city. Their inclusion in almost every burgh (sometimes in a variant cottage version) is a witness to their appeal, even if in some places they are represented by handfuls rather than streets. There were three factors involved: being smaller, they were a cheap entry into the property market by the lower middle classes who became established in the inter-war years; they were a symbol of privacy, being detached and what one observer calls 'territorially separate'; and they emulated the values associated with country house ownership.

One interesting thread in the history of suburban architecture in Scotland is the fact that, despite the use of mass-produced motifs and the free market economy in which builders operated, there is still a distinctively Scottish character to the suburbs, at least up to World War Two and what has been called the burgeoning Wimpeylands of recent years. This is partly due to the continued use of stone and stone facing in building, and the urge, where brick is used, to cover it with harling (in contrast to English habit). Scottish brick was of poor quality, though extensively used in the interior of tenements. Adams (1978) saw a prejudice against brick demonstrated by 'the startling difference between stone-built Langholm and the brick townscape of Carlisle, a mere 30 km away. . . .' Even a concept as English as the brick bungalow is translated into a stone-faced version – Aberdeen even boasts the granite bungalow – though the Scottish reinterpretation does not always meet with approval. Naismith (1989) finds that 'the Scottish builders did not understand the need for the roads to be in scale with the bungalows, which are of small hamlet scale and not suited to long suburban roads'. The fact that the standard Scottish road was wider than the English aggravated the effect. The scarcity of wood in many parts has also contributed to the absence in Scotland of the 'jacobethan' extravagances of bargeboard facing that dominate many an English town. Another factor was that private suburban development was much less extensive in Scotland (especially in the inter-war years), and was consequently more easily drawn into its sturdy architectural tradition. Perhaps too, a native sense of restraint, a natural concomitant of an austere environment, has played its part.

The council house movement

Adams (1978) recorded that since 1919 over 1,200,000 permanent homes had been built in Scotland, of which over 950,000 were in the public sector. In some towns the proportion of council housing has been quite overwhelming – over 80 per cent in Airdrie, Kilsyth and Coatbridge, and over 70 per cent in Lochgelly, Motherwell and Wishaw and Port Glasgow. Stevenston, Cowdenbeath, Johnstone and Falkirk have figures of over 60 per cent. The preconditions for this lay in the failure of nineteenth-century market forces to provide adequate housing for the working classes. Considerable fluctuations in the building cycle were noted even by contemporaries, and in bad times, such as just prior to the First World War, building almost came to a standstill. From the peak year of 1876 when around 29,000 houses were constructed, the figure slumped to around 7,000 in 1879; only again reached 20,000 in 1900, and fell to the nadir of under 5,000 in 1912 and 1913. The crisis of that decade provoked the establishment of the Royal Commission on Housing in Scotland, which reported to parliament in 1916. The condition of housing in Scotland was 'a standing disgrace to the nation', it reported, with 113,430 uninhabitable properties and 47.9 per cent of the population in houses of one or two rooms (the English figure was 7.1 per cent).

The commissioners gave graphic descriptions of conditions in these houses: 'In Greenock a case was found in which fifty-four persons were using one water-closet. An overflow from a water-closet caused walls to crack and a ceiling to collapse three times in six months'. No wonder it can be written that the slum was 'the main contribution of the Victorian Age to architecture' (Jordan, 1966).

It was increasingly argued, against the optimism of the Victorian age, that market forces were essentially incapable of solving the problems of housing the poor. The high feu duties have already been noted. As a result, the Commission found, 'the working man in cities pays a very much greater sum for the land on which his house stands than the man in the well-to-do villa'. High feu duties were matched by low wages. In the 1830s bricklayers had earned 25 per cent less in Edinburgh than in Birmingham; the discrepancy was still in the order of 16–19 per cent in the 1860s and parity had not been reached by the twentieth century. To compound the inequality, prices were higher. The invisible hand of such market forces vitiated even the good intentions of public housing authorities after the First World War, and indeed continues to thwart efforts to ameliorate Scotland's housing stock to this day.

The pioneers of non-market-sponsored housing grappled quite unsuccessfully with the problems. Most important were the improvement trusts set up by local acts of parliament in the cities, under the sponsorship of the local authorities, in the 1860s. The Glasgow City Improvement Trust was the first and most well-known, but whilst it superintended the demolition of whole areas of slums, it caused very little to be built in their place (1,646 houses between 1866 and 1902), thus exacerbating the overcrowding elsewhere. Philanthropic cooperative ventures were no more successful and served to prove the point that only the élite artisanal wing of the working class was sufficiently affluent and sufficiently secure in regular employment to take on the burden of either home ownership or higher rents. Similar problems bedevilled good quality council house provision after the First World War. Edinburgh's Cooperative Building Company was a model for similar agencies in Hawick, Grangemouth and Dalkeith.

Some housing improvements did occur in the first decade of the century. Coal companies such as the Edinburgh Collieries Company built improved miners' cottages with small patches of garden ground at the front to replace the old rows opening on to muddy untarred roads. Even better three- and four-apartment houses followed from such as William Baird and Company who built a total of 3,464 homes in mining towns, including Bathgate and Kilwinning. The pre-First World War rearmament programme was responsible for a pioneering development at Rosyth, where the Admiralty built a new town on 'garden city' lines. The garden city was another manifestation of the country in the town principle, inspired by Ebenezer Howard. The idea was taken up by the Scottish Veterans' Garden City Association, founded in 1915 to provide homes 'fit for heroes'. It built several hundred houses.

Despite these piecemeal developments, the general view endorsed by the Royal Commission on Housing was that 'no satisfactory programme of housing can be carried out unless a definite obligation is placed on some person or Authority to see that a sufficient number of suitable houses is systematically provided'. That obligation fell, in 1919, firmly on the shoulders of local authorities (town and county councils). Local government powers of intervention in the housing market dated as far back as the 1850s, when the Dwelling Houses (Scotland) Act and Nuisances Removal Act respectively sanctioned compulsory purchase of dilapidated property and laid down obligations for maintaining premises in habitable condition. Direct ventures into public housing were restricted, and included some council-owned lodging houses for the considerable number of immigrants, migrant workers and vagrants who tramped from one end of the country to the other. A concerted effort to control overcrowding in the many privately-owned lodging houses led to Glasgow's innovatory ticketing system, the number of permitted lodgers being fixed to the outside wall. The underlying philosophy, based on concern for the morality of overcrowding, not its dangers to health and welfare (a good example of the control of the social space of towns by its élite) was widely copied, and books and posters of lodging house rules can be found in the records of many towns.

The significance of the 1919 Housing (Scotland) Act, known as the Addison Act, was twofold: that it made council building obligatory, and that it introduced general subsidy. High standards were again inspired by the garden city ideal. The Tudor Walters report of 1918, which preceded the act, had recommended a maximum density of 12 houses per acre, arranged in cul de sacs around open spaces. The houses were to be grouped in terraces of four to six. Linked garden walls and tunnels providing access to rear gardens are also to be found on estates which closely followed the garden city ideas. The strictest conditions of all were probably those insisted on by Sir John Stirling Maxwell, who sold his Nether Pollok estate to Glasgow Town Council on condition that stringent architectural and social criteria were met. Glasgow built other garden suburbs of its own volition (Riddrie, Mosspark, Knightswood), as did numerous other councils, including Alva (Minto Gardens designed by William Kerr in 1919) and Dundee (Craigie Garden Suburb).

The shaky foundations of these utopian projects were exposed by the problem of unaffordable rents already alluded to; but that problem paled into insignificance alongside the crisis caused by the country's bankrupt economy of the inter-war years. Housing acts followed each other almost yearly as conservative, socialist and nationalist governments in turn wrestled with free market and subsidy philosophies against a background of economic recession. In no year through the 1920s were more than 10,000 houses built in Scotland; in the 1930s an average of over 15,000 was maintained, but at the cost of reduced quality and considerable increase in density levels.

The traditional stone-built council houses from the early halcyon days are easy to spot today. They were soon replaced by the distinctive harling and brick to be found in every town in Scotland – Bearsden is exceptional, with under five per cent of its housing stock council built. At the other extreme is Clydebank, in which *private* building accounted for less than five per cent of inter-war development. The similarity of house design across Scotland is due to the use of standard plans from the Local Government Board, originally prepared in connection with the housing of the working class acts 1890–1909. As with bungaloid growth, some architectural historians have seen the introduction of cottage styles in garden settings as an intrusion of alien English cultural traditions, even with the addition of Scots decorative features such as crow-stepped gables. The best of the estates, such as the Lucy Sanderson Homes in Galashiels, have, however, mellowed into the Scottish town scene. The economical building of the 1930s reverted more to tenement traditions, though the favoured reinterpretation, of a flatted two-storey block of four houses (making the houses higher than their English counterparts) set in the wider standard road of 20 feet, contributed to the mechanical appearance of council estates.

It is interesting to note, none the less, that, unlike the speculative building of middle-class suburbs, council estates were usually planned as a conceptual whole. Some have attacked the depressing similarity that results. For example, the 1948 Committee on the Appearance of Housing Estates criticized the 'dull straight rows' and the 'severe, geometrical road patterns which bear no relation to the underlying landscape features'. It is instructive that the same criticisms have been levelled at the generally admired Georgian townscapes; and the two developments share the involvement of a professional élite of architects and planners with a philosophy in direct contrast to that of spec builders. The unity of style in council estates has found its advocates, who doubtless deplore the personalization of the houses that has occurred since the recent council-house selling movement, just as they would deplore an intrusively bright painted door in a Georgian terrace.

The failure of inter-war governments to solve the housing crisis was compounded by the destruction and neglect caused by World War Two. The post-war years (which have seen a dramatic doubling in the number of households) have witnessed a determined effort, with 11 major housing acts between 1945 and 1970. Improvements were sought both in quality and quantity, and various responses made to criticisms of the monotony of council housing. Mixed development schemes appeared, attention was redirected to the rehabilitation of decaying town centres, and a new form of estate layout abandoning orthodox street frontages became popular.

Flatted accommodation of four-storey blocks maintained the tenement tradition, but pressure on funds and space led to a new high-rise solution. Construction of tower blocks was restricted mainly to the big cities. Glasgow, with its severe land shortage, was committed to this building type from the late 1950s, and 163 skyscrapers were occupied by the end of the next decade.

Another response to the post-war problem was the monster suburb, complete with its own neighbourhood shopping centres and communal services of schools, libraries, churches, swimming baths, cinemas, clinics and parks. Glasgow's Castlemilk (started in 1953) and Pollok (actually conceived before the war with a projected 8,300 homes) made the common mistake of building the houses first so that urban blight set in even before the scheme was completed. The original plan, mainly featuring three-storey tenements of three apartments, was amended to include 20-storey tower blocks.

A more radical solution, addressed specifically to Glasgow's problems, was the creation of new towns virtually from scratch. Gretna has been considered Scotland's first government-sponsored new town, with its First World War garden city scheme. The scale of its concept was tiny in comparison with the 1950s plan to displace half a million people from Glasgow. Of the various sites proposed, those eventually designated new towns were East Kilbride (population 71,737 in 1981), Glenrothes (32,747), Cumbernauld (48,413), Irvine (55,436) and Livingston (36,920). Glasgow overspill was also absorbed by existing towns under special agreements made with Glasgow Town Council.

Another important post-war movement has been the work of the Scottish Special Housing Association (now Scottish Homes), which built over 89,000 houses between 1945 and 1985. Its declared aim was to compensate for the shortfall in local authority housing. Unlike conventional housing associations it has been, broadly speaking, controlled by government. One of its strategies has been experimentation with new building materials and methods such as timber, prefabricated brick and 'no firer' (sand-free) concrete. Local councils have also experimented. In the inter-war years Clydebank used concrete blocks for its first scheme at East Kilbowie, and steel-framed and steel-walled construction ('the Atholl steel house'). 'Buildings constructed of concrete blocks *improve* with age – the concrete hardening with exposure' claims the post-World War One advertising of William Bain and Co. of Coatbridge. Prefabrication of different types was an urgent response to the post-war housing crisis. The enforced simplicity of style today begins to take on a period character, as do the Scandinavian-inspired pine-bedecked homes of the 1960s with their multiple steep-pitched roofs. The many flat-roofed experiments have proved none too resistant to the Scottish climate, and today are often converted to pitched roofs. The flat-roof phenomenon has also afflicted a multitude of public buildings.

Housing interiors

Of the interior of the one-roomed tenement flat, once so prevalent in Scotland, little can be said. 'It is a constant succession of lifting, folding, and hanging up, and if this is relaxed for even a short time the confusion is overwhelming' notes the Royal Commission on Housing in 1916. It was as if, suggest McKean and Walker (1985), 'the but-and-ben cottages familiar to rural immigrants were set on top of one another instead of end-to-end'. The stress was never greater than at times of death: 'The beloved dead is laid on the bed, and all the usual round of domestic duties, including the taking of meals, has to be done with ever that still, pale form before their view. Night comes on, and the household must go to rest, so the sad burden is now transferred from the bed and laid on the table, or it may be the coal-bunker lid.' Evenings in the tenements saw children forced out of doors to allow the wife space to do housework. The Rev. Dr Watson of Glasgow reported to the Royal Commission that 'in my evening visitation I find the children everywhere – sitting in the closes and on the stairs, trying to play, often half-asleep, on bitter winter nights'.

The larger tenement houses were by no means unpleasant to live in, though jerrybuilding tended to coincide with periods of boom. 'The carpentry or joiner's work of these four or five storey flats need no description' claims the *Builder* of 26 March 1870, 'It might have been executed by an amateur casual'. Adams (1978) suggests that 'small investors demanded structural strength, but showed little concern for the internal layout of the houses'.

The ethos of the Victorian suburban home demanded that it should aim to 'comfort and purify, to give relief and privacy from the cares of the world, to rear its members in an appropriate set of Christian values, and above all, to proclaim by its ordered arrangements, polite behaviour, cleanliness, tidiness and distinctive taste that its members belonged to a class of substance, culture and respectability' (Burnett, 1980). Feminization of the home was reflected in a clutter of embroidery and ornament – symbols of the domestic skills of a wife whose status symbol was her spare time. Within the clutter, suggests Simpson (1977), 'a harmonium or baby grand piano was universal, and later in the century a Singer sewing machine occupied one of the alcoves. Edwardian households dispensed with stuffed birds, antlers and engravings in favour of family photographs'.

The basic layout of the Victorian house remained similar to that established in Georgian times, with separate access to every room, though a new consciousness of sanitary issues led to better ventilation and higher ceilings. Basements disappeared, the kitchen and sculleries moving to a rear annexe next to an outside privy, with an extra bedroom on the floor above. Bathrooms came on to the scene with technological advances in circulatory hot water systems in the 1870s, incidentally stimulating a passion for the hygienic wall tile also found in food shops of the time. Flushing loos were uncommon owing to the general lack of mains sewerage. Where it was found, notes Barrett and Phillips (1987), 'the porcelain handle . . . at the end of the chain usually had the word "pull" written on it, to save the embarrassment of the house guest who had not come across such a novelty before'. The introduction of compulsory WCs in the Burgh Police (Scotland) Act 1892 led to WC stacks being added to working-class tenements in the form of four-storey towers, usually of brick, with a single WC for communal use on each landing.

Before the First World War, rooms were small even in fairly large houses, so that different functions could be segregated as in the houses of the gentry (smoking rooms, billiard rooms etc). Working-class housing in its turn cultivated (even up to recent times) the front room or parlour reserved for the formal visit, though probably less in Scotland than in England. Considerations of prestige were also responsible for the imposing front entrances of Victorian houses, with their porches and pillars still being copied by spec builders in the inter-war years. Hallways were grander than we find today, for here the guests waited before being shepherded into the sacred heart of the house, the drawing room. A more cramped version was the hall staircase with two quarter turns and a landing to accommodate what Barrett and Phillips (1987) call 'a minuscule "gallery" . . . symbolically important vestiges of baronial halls . . .'

The decline in the number of servants had a considerable impact on house design, both in the loss of provision for living-in and an increased emphasis on time-saving features. A subtle shift in priority is also discernible, from 'the house as a place primarily for the display and ritual observances of its adult occupants' to one 'for the rational use and recreation of all its members' (Burnett, 1978). The emphasis on naturalness encouraged a fresh air and sunshine philosophy, already noted for being a source of inspiration behind the bungalow. Maximization of sunlight was a feature of post-1918 council house design, in which projecting back extensions for kitchen and toilet were taboo – sunlight was to shine directly into as many rooms as possible. Three bedrooms and two living rooms (plus scullery) were regarded as the minimum; larders and bathrooms essential. The espousal of flat-roofed housing was also based on the premise that they allowed more sunlight to reach inside – Glasgow accordingly built 500 such houses at Carntyre.

The importance attached to light and convenience led to another innovation: open planning, with kitchen/living room combined – the 'forced bonhomie of open plan living' as a character in Alice Thomas Ellis's novel *The Sin Eater* puts it. This functional idea was reluctantly taken up by private builders, who persisted (with a sound insight into the pretensions of their clientele) in designing homes divided into rooms for receiving guests and rooms where the routine of day-to-day living was maintained. Bungalows were more flexible, their success being partly due to their solution of the servant problem: 'the single-storey plan . . . the simple furnishing, serving hatch between kitchen and dining room with sideboard underneath . . . and the emphasis on "the least amount of household work" were portents which would explain the bungalow's future success' claims King (1984).

Post-Second World War developments were minutely analysed in the Parker Morris Report of 1961, which drew attention to the advantages of an eating space in the kitchen area. It marks the culminating point in the apotheosis of the kitchen from, in Burnett's (1978) words, 'the cheerless

Victorian scullery to the centre of household activity, skilfully planned, equipped with labour saving devices and often furnished as a room where at least some family meals are normally eaten'. The *News of the World Better Homes Book* of 1954 could still talk of 'a tastefully planned home' providing 'a wife with a graceful background and a haven for the husband, where business worries can be temporarily banished' – words which could as well be from a different century, for the working wife of the 1960s. These recent decades have also witnessed a growing classlessness of house design, with little difference between council housing and the private housing which once attempted to look as different as could be.

Studying the interiors of local houses can make an interesting project for local historians. There are problems – the likelihood of substantial alteration to older property, certainly in the decor, and the absence of contemporary photographic record. Even after the invention of flash, there is little visual record of interiors, as few people have stopped to think of the historical significance of familiar domestic surroundings. A valuable contribution by a local history society would be the systematic photographing of a representative sample from the interiors of a town's housing stock. It is chastening to reflect that this is one aspect of urban experience and urban space which has been omitted almost completely from historical scrutiny.

Alterations to layout are not an insurmountable problem. Kitchen annexes and the like are usually betrayed by variation in stonework or finish, and subsequent partitioning has a way of betraying itself too under close observation. Original plans can be found in the Dean of Guild Approved Duplicate Plans and Minute Books, and for the contents of houses there is a major documentary source in the inventories drawn up in connection with testamentary procedures. Scots law distinguished until recently between the disposal on death of heritable property (mainly land) and movable property (goods). The latter since 1823 has come under the jurisdiction of the sheriff courts, in their commissary capacity (prior to 1823 special commissary courts had supervised inheritance). In Scots law it has been incumbent for centuries upon the executor of an estate to draw up an inventory of all the movable property, to be deposited with the court together with the will (if one exists). If there is a will the procedure is known as *testament testamentary*; if not *testament dative*. The information is duly entered in the court's register of testaments. Sheriff court records are mostly deposited in the Scottish Record Office, where the inventories can be consulted. Finding aids include a printed *Index to Personal Estates of Defuncts* (covering the Lothians 1827–65 and other areas 1846–67) and, from 1876, an annual printed *Calendar of Confirmations and Inventories, Granted and Given by the Seven Commissariots of Scotland*.

Research ideas and sources

The local historian who chooses to study the housing of his or her town should be aware of the economic conditions which have dictated its form, quality and situation. Rodger (1975) noted that towns dominated by a single industry such as the iron and steel burghs of Motherwell, Wishaw, Coatbridge, Airdrie and Falkirk, and the textile centres of Hawick and Galashiels, show quite clearly how interrelated are industrial performance and house building. During periods of rapid business expansion, the incidence of cheap jerry-built housing is high; contraction is followed by a rise in the number of empty properties, little housebuilding and bankruptcy among tradesmen. Where the contraction is considerable, the repercussions can be as serious as complete stagnation in a town's evolution for a whole generation. In Galashiels, for instance, the depression of 1890–1908 reduced the population by 3,600, leaving empty accommodation sufficient to depress house building even through the inter-war years. 'Only the Forest Gardens estate', adds Rodger, 'built under the subsidy arrangements, and some installation of WCs to remedy the deficient standards tolerated during the 1880s boom, provided employment for building workers'.

Other local circumstances to be considered are the level of rents and the demand caused by immigration and lowered levels of mortality, which can be studied through the valuation rolls and the published decennial census reports respectively. Building costs are another factor: there is a surprisingly wide variation, with Aberdeen's cost per cubic foot for a block of two cottages being 50 per cent higher than Glasgow's in the Victorian period. Against these local factors must also be balanced macro-economic forces, expressed in the view that transatlantic movements of people and capital affect the building programmes of the smallest burgh. The theory has been summed up in the aphorism that 'it was the prosperity of the Dakotas, so to speak, that brought building to a standstill in Dalmarnock' (quoted in Rodger, 1975).

Architectural studies of a town's housing are difficult, in inverse proportion to their architectural significance. Every listed building (A, B or C category as allocated by the Scottish Development Department) will be described in the town's published list of *Buildings of Architectural or Historical Interest*, originally produced by the Scottish Home and Health Department. However, the entry may be nothing more than a vague date attribution. Major listed buildings, being part of the nation's architectural heritage, have been carefully recorded by the Royal Commission on Ancient and Historical Monuments for Scotland, and published in inventories organized on a county basis since 1909 (though the series is still not completed). At its National Monuments Record Office in Coates Place, Edinburgh, the Royal Commission keeps many of its notes and records available for public consultation. The architectural section includes a huge collection of photographs, old and new, arranged by Region, plus plans, indexes and information files. The Index of Scottish Architects brings together published and unpublished sources. Information about architects is also contained in some of the volumes of architectural history published in the last few years jointly by the Royal Incorporation of Architects in Scotland and the Scottish Academic Press. This series (now covering several areas and cities) has been justly acclaimed; it is unmatched and indispensable, both for its interest in the everyday domestic environment, and in its enthusiasm for the odd and ordinary as much as for the aesthetically exceptional. Its nearest rivals are the Pevsner-inspired Penguin guides, of which only a few have so far appeared for Scottish areas. Architectural drawings and plans are to be found in a variety of other locations – library and museum local history collections, the National Library of Scotland, the Scottish Record Office (West Register House), architects' offices, and English institutions such as the British Architectural Library (at the RIBA).

For the standard suburban house of the last century and a half, there will be less chance of finding information outside the Dean of Guild and valuation sources discussed in the last chapter. Nineteenth-century properties are sometimes documented in the records of the fire insurance companies, some of whom provided a fire brigade service – but only to those premises displaying their plaques. The early trade journals

The Builder (1842–) and *Building News* (1855–) are a marvellous source, though of more value to the historian seeking an overview than one wanting to trace the history of a particular house or street. An ongoing project to index all pictorial references in the *Builder* between 1842 and 1883 will be a great boon. It is discussed in *The Local Studies Librarian* Volume 9, no. 1, Spring 1990, pp. 13–15. Local government archives apart from Dean of Guild records will be useful, particularly for the history of council housing and the more recent planning-conscious era. A frequent survival are the various registers kept from the 1920s and 1930s – of new houses built, of council tenants, of overcrowded houses and of those unfit for habitation. Scottish Office records are housed in the West Register House of the Scottish Record Office. The files of the Home and Health Department (previously two separate departments) and Scottish Development Department are the most relevant. Because of the great amount of papers generated by government, much weeding has had to take place, so that many local files are retained as samples of the types of activity sponsored by government (for example the files for housing conditions in selected burghs in 1925, inventory DD6). A two-volume information pack, *Housing in Strathkelvin*, published by Strathkelvin District Libraries and Museums, 1989, includes facsimiles of many types of document as well as reminiscences and newspaper reports – a marvellous source of ideas for researchers in other localities.

The most revealing analysts of the domestic scene are, naturally enough, its inhabitants. Unfortunately we cannot interrogate our Victorian forebears, though we can seek out the comments they made to parliamentary commissioners. Novels, too, tell us something of the domestic side of life, and can indeed be used to garner a range of perceptions on Scottish urban life. Collecting memories of housing conditions on tape and video can give a picture of twentieth-century developments. Questions can probe beyond the physical conditions, furnishings and organization of domestic labour to the value placed on home life, the aspirations of the occupants, the behaviour of landlords public and private, and attitudes towards the neighbourhood.

Chapter Four

THE BUSINESS OF A TOWN

A crucial factor in the development of towns is the constant tension between an organizing authority (a state or local council) and the interests of individuals and groups who are, to a greater or lesser extent, subject to its powers. It has been argued that the taxes imposed on entrepreneurs to finance the council house programme needed for the preservation of a fragile social stability (and a work force for the entrepreneurs) crippled business development. Similarly, new departures and new locations for industry have been restricted by the reduction in labour mobility caused by massive public housing provision in areas of declining economic viability. The inertia drag of towns is constant – most people live where they do merely because their parents and grandparents lived there, sometimes long after the original economic justification has been forgotten. A town can be regarded as a well-preserved or not so well-preserved graveyard of former opportunities, or the concrete detritus of long-past market forces.

The two poles of the public framework and private initiative are the subject of the present and following chapters. However, whatever the special characteristics of individual towns which have contributed to their unique personality, the private market-oriented facet is the one which ultimately prevails. All towns are spatially organized round concentrations of job opportunities, business and retail services, and the urban transportation network which facilitates their operation.

In contrast to the seemingly anarchic growth of towns in the nineteenth century, most urban centres were originally planned and planted in accordance with public policy. The similarity of their core structure certainly suggests as much. The most common form was a wide, straight or slightly curving street (Edinburgh, Musselburgh, Montrose, Elgin) or a variant which produced a more wedge-shaped, semi-enclosed central area (Haddington, Stirling, Dundee, Dumfries). The original wedge shape is now usually obscured by the process known as market colonization – the building of island sites within the open area. The poorer, less important burghs can sometimes be recognized by the narrowness of their central high streets.

The importance of the market is the key to the strategy of the towns' founders – in the case of the old burghs usually the king. The raison d'être was the development and exploitation of trade in favour of both the crown itself (needing levies for central government functions such as national protection) and its privileged allies within the burghs – the burgessses – many of whom may initially have been deliberately settled foreigners. The burgesses formed the community of the burgh and monopolized its political and economic control.

It is axiomatic that any power structure depends for its survival on an unequal distribution of rights and opportunities. In the case of towns, the inequality was at the expense of the non-burgess inhabitants, but it was probably even more to the detriment of the inhabitants of the rural hinterland. From the latter's point of view, the advantage of a central market was limited, as most of the products (food and its derivatives) came from that hinterland, with minimal industrial processing.

Each royal burgh was surrounded by its liberties, whose boundaries in the lowlands extended to where they met those of the neighbouring burgh. All trade and exchange of raw and manufactured goods had to be transacted in the burgh market place, at a price fixed by the authorities and subject to market tolls. Posters listing the tax on a range of items are common survivals in council archives. From the seventeenth century the general markets diversified according to product, with the most important taking the best locations: the flesh markets, for example, needed vennels with good drainage slopes. Other products included salt, leather, meal, butter and cheese. Some local open-air markets persisted in the industrial towns.

Retailing

We now take it for granted that the central area of a town is dominated by shops; and the reason for this dominance is crucial to an understanding of how towns work. For it was not always the case. Edinburgh New Town, when completed, had no provision for shops at all. By 1800 there were some 18 at street level in Princes Street, with small frontages. Lord Cockburn's *Memorials of His Time* (1856) recall that 'the dislike of them was so great, that any proprietor who allowed one was abused as an unneighbourly fellow'. By 1850 most of the ground floors had been taken over, and by 1900 only one integral dwelling house remained, by which time the existing shops were rapidly expanding upwards and outwards in what Naismith (1989) calls its 'land of hope and glory' architecture. By 1960 Moray McLaren was describing it as 'one of the most chaotically tasteless streets in the United Kingdom' (quoted in McKean and Walker, 1983). The demands of retailing, it seems, sweep aside everything in their path, be it domestic peace, civic grandeur or religious monument.

The absence of shops would have been quite unremarked by the medieval, or even by the seventeenth-century, town dweller. Retailing or regrating was in fact an offence against the economic rules of the town, as was forestalling (literally, making a sale before reaching the market area). The retailer – he who bought only to sell again – was execrated for monopolizing a market by buying up disproportionate amounts of a scarce product. There was no place for such a man in an impoverished economy, where trade was pre-dominantly in food products and animal derivatives. Even in nineteenth-century cities, according to Davis (1966), there was 'an immediate connection, now quite lost sight of, between the food on the table and the surrounding country-side'. Butchers, for example, kept their cattle in fields on the outskirts and brought them in daily to a centrally-situated slaughter house. Davis also refers to dairymen, 'who kept their cows in cellars or at the back of their shops, often in appallingly dirty and primitive conditions'. Such small dairies persisted into this century, to become victims of anti-tuberculosis legislation. Foodstuff and other markets of course still survive, and account for a proportion of retail trade, even though changing pressures on town centre use may have pushed them out of the central, prestigious area which they were instrumental in founding and shaping. Many nineteenth-century towns built special covered premises for new markets; particularly notable in this respect is Aberdeen, which covered its ancient Green with the New Market (1840–2) – no less than 100 metres' length of enclosed space.

The economics of scarcity may have continued to justify medieval controls in food marketing – 'the seller's market' in the words of Davis (1966) – but in other areas they became increasingly irrelevant. How irrelevant can be gauged by the mounting corruption of the town councils which underpinned the controls. When an institution defends principles which are no longer tenable, its isolation is very likely to create an embattled élite desperate to maintain privileges. Such was the situation in burghs prior to their reform in the 1830s.

The impetus for change came partly from the introduction of new, non-animal based products such as watches and partly from imported food products (spices, coffee, tea) for which an open market had much less relevance. Such goods had initially featured at fairs, whither they were carried by pedlars and merchants. However, with the growth in the size of towns and the incipient demand for luxury goods, especially dress and accessories from the socially top heavy towns such as Edinburgh, the persecuted retailer came into his own. Two significant breaks from the past occurred: permanent shops appeared (with all the overheads attendant on a fixed site, for which of course the consumer must ultimately pay); and the identity between producer and seller was severed. A retailer did not fashion or grow his product.

Initially there was no corresponding split between whole-saler and retailer: the warehouses of the successful burghal merchants were also their shops, as was noted by Edward Burt in his *Letters from the Highlands* in 1722: 'There is, indeed, a Shop up a Pair of Stairs, which is kept by three or four Merchants in Partnership, and that is pretty well stored with various Sorts of small Goods and Wares, mostly from London. This shop is called, by Way of Eminence, the Warehouse . . .'. Burt's shop was in Inverness. An Alyth (Perthshire) merchant's stock in trade recorded in the bank-ruptcy papers 75 years later includes silver watches, snuff, buttons, tea, black tea, writing books, gloves, mahogany dining tables, a hat, hose, duffel, lawn, muslin, serge, shirting, forest cloth, gauze, cambric, gingham, velveteen, sugar, breeches and Emley hogshead, none of which emana-ted from the local economy. Many early twentieth-century shops still called themselves warehouses.

The modern High Street began to take shape around the middle of the nineteenth century, when small towns like Alyth were introduced to the specialist shop. Initially the street would have been composed of small shops of single plot width – indeed, we sometimes forget that even today, the majority of shops are no bigger. Some shopkeepers – butchers have already been mentioned, but we can add shoemakers, bakers, tailors, ale-sellers, blacksmiths, spirit sellers – retained the medieval link between producer and retailer. Food traders in particular merely transferred their operation from stall to shop, the advantage being day-long accessibility, the disadvantage the need for permanent staffing. The introduction of gas lighting increased the economic potential of the shop.

The number and distribution of these small shops can be studied in local directories and in the burgh valuation rolls from the mid-1850s. An earlier, eighteenth-century, tax record is the Shop Tax Assessments held in the Scottish Record Office (the rate depended upon shop size, as assessed by government officers). The large number is understandable when we remember that there was no public transport and little private transport. They also feature prominently in many of those nineteenth-century burgh histories full of stories about old characters, of whom one is invariably, as Davis (1966) suggests, 'an old dame who sold home-made boiled sweets'. The interest in shops and what they sold remains strong today, being linked to the pleasure of childhood memories; reminiscence and oral history publications are full of examples, as in Nessie Marshall's detailed recall of Selkirk's main street in *A Pennyworth o' Elephant's Tiptaes*. As was noted in Chapter 2, the shopkeeping fraternity was instrumental in financing much of the housing development in towns, a process which a study of valuation rolls will also reveal. Dubbed the 'shopocracy', they were prominent in local politics, at least up to the time of local government reorganization in 1974.

Though the independent shopkeeper has proved enduring, and has continued to prosper through diversification (Davis observes that the grocer now sells wrapped bread, tights and cigarettes), he or she has had to face competition from several large-scale retailing initiatives since the mid-nineteenth century. In many respects, industrialization made the skilled craftsman/retailer redundant, ending the days of the apprentice and opening the door to managerialism. 'Melrose tea, sold in sealed packets bearing our signature' run the newspaper advertisements of an Edinburgh wholesaler at the turn of the century. Formerly, even a retailer such as a grocer had undertaken skilled functions in tea blending and preparation of hams, but the growth of proprietory brands, canned products and industrial manufacture switched attention to the mass movement of goods, economies of scale and standardized quantities.

The new techniques were seized upon by the co-operative movement, whose true innovatory nature as far as retailing is concerned has been obscured by the interest shown in its social theories of dividend and democratic ownership. The co-operative revolution lies in two other aspects, its vertical integration and its branch store policy. Vertical integration refers to the practice of bulk wholesaling, under the aegis of the Scottish Co-operative Wholesale Society (founded 1868), from whom the local societies bought their goods. The establishment of branches was the novel solution to the expansionary pressures of a successful business. With these two weapons and the bolstering of demand from a working class benefiting from an improvement in their living standards, the success of the movement was assured. The taste of the working classes for mass-produced foodstuffs served only to reinforce the logic of the wholesaling strategy.

Co-operative retailing began in earnest in small towns and villages in the 1860s, with an early concentration on the grocery trade and to the great alarm of private shopkeepers. In West Calder (Midlothian) the latter set up a bakery in 1886 selling bread at cost price to attract trade away from the successful West Calder Co-operative (which numbered 5,728 members in 1913 in a parish with a population of 7,716). Marshall (1984) recalled a Selkirk butcher with 'a great antipathy to the Store as the co-operative was usually known. He often opened his shop at a holiday but if you were sent for sausages, you were quite likely to be greeted with "Is yer mither a member o' the Store? Weel tell her tae git her sausages where she gits the rest o' hir meat" '. Competition between different societies was avoided through the efforts of the Co-operative Union.

Consolidation occurred after the First World War with membership up to one in five of the population. The period also saw the amalgamation of many of the town and village co-operatives into larger conglomerates, allowing ventures into factory production, large-scale dairying and laundering, and the multiplication of specialist stores, for hardware, drapery, shoes and furniture. The long-term weakness of these was their organization under the direction of individual societies rather than through specialist national networks. In other respects, their democratic management and near-monopoly in many industrial towns (especially mining communities) acted as a drag on innovation and encouraged uncompetitive pricing. In 1945 Anders Hedberg of the Swedish Co-operative Union found on a Scottish visit that 'where the co-operative shops dominate, the society naturally determines what prices shall be current thereabouts. . . . Proposals to reduce prices and dividends have often been discussed in many societies but met strenuous opposition from members'. In other words, the incentive of high dividends as a savings investment for the better-off workers was maintained at the expense of the poor who could not afford to save.

The specialist networks which the co-operatives failed to develop on a national basis were successfully established by private companies, and this phenomenon became the second major retailing development of the Victorian age. Multiple chain retailing was pioneered (1870–90) in footwear, butchery, grocery and newspapers, with hardware, tobacco, clothing and chemists' goods following behind. One Scottish pioneer was Thomas Lipton who started a one-man grocery shop in Glasgow in 1872. Twenty-six years later, there were 245 'Lipton's Markets' – the name was chosen to emphasize cheapness – achieving economies of scale through concentration on a few basic foodstuffs. The market image was also the catalyst for the Penny Bazaars of Marks and Spencer and Woolworth. By 1914 there was no important area of retailing from which multiple shops were absent; 16 firms had over 200 branches each throughout the United Kingdom, and seven of them had over 500 branches. Their astonishing success was, as with the co-operatives, rooted in working-class patronage, for whom they developed 'a system of mass distribution with the minimum of frills to parallel the growth of large-scale production and the bulked imports of standardized goods' (Jefferys, 1954). It is interesting to note, with Davis (1966), that here 'the poorer sections of the community led the way and the fashion spread upwards' – a reversal of the often-noticed percolation of fashion *down* the social scale.

A revolution in selling techniques went hand in hand with multiple retailing. The emergence of brand labels and manufacturers' advertising led to a policy of price fixing, and (even more vulgar in contemporary eyes) price labelling. R. K. Philp's *Handybook of Shopkeeping* of 1892 notes that 'In Edinburgh, as in London, higgling is now gone out of date in all respectable establishments and so it is in Glasgow. Formerly no one could enter a haberdasher's shop in the cities without spending half-an-hour or so in higgling with the shopkeeper'. A shopkeeper selling pre-packaged goods, with no knowledge of or competence in the contents, would have been at a loss to know how to haggle.

The success of multiples has been enduring, both in their traditional fields, with conglomerates such as the Home and Colonial Grocery Group building an empire of over 3,000 shops in the United Kingdom in the inter-war years, and in new fields of consumer goods attendant upon technological advances and increasing affluence (areas such as electrical goods, radio, cars and toiletries). Multiple trading both encouraged and responded to 'style' in consumer behaviour, a marketing-led process which caused shops to change from 'units that existed solely to fulfil customers' wants to units designed and planned to attract customers and create wants' (Jefferys, 1954). The consequences for High Street architecture were considerable, as will be discussed below.

The third pillar of the retailing revolution of the mid-nineteenth century was the arrival, from France, of the department store. Starting from the humble base of a traditional shop, the ambitious proprietor bought up adjacent lots until a complete street block or island site was acquired, with the dual advantage of providing more space and eliminating local competition. Whereas multiples succeeded through economies of scale, department stores exploited economies of location, making available an enormous range of items within a relatively small space. The preferred strategy was the creation of an ambience of glamour for the sale of cheap goods (particularly fashion goods) – exactly the same trick as has been used successfully in advertising in our own time, After Eight Mints being a classic example. Flattery of the emerging nineteenth-century middle classes by an army of liftmen, doormen, shopwalkers and vanmen provided the sort of attention the aristocracy had traditionally expected from its servants. Department stores have tended to retain their local individuality, even when absorbed by national conglomerates. Scottish examples are John Anderson's in Glasgow and Jenners in Edinburgh.

The High Street and its architecture

Even in the smallest towns the High Street is a dominant presence, and one which influences our mental picture of a town more than any other feature. Retailing has been its prime activity in the last 150 years, so it is important to find explanations of why this should be. The answer lies in the philosophy of capitalism which replaced the traditional market organization discussed earlier in this chapter. For capitalism, the medieval *bêtes noires* of individual accumulation and defiance of any supervising authority were deemed to be, on the contrary, economic virtues, the only regulatory force approved being free market competition. As a result, the civic character of the town centre, hitherto symbolic, in its vernacular uniformity, of the communal ideology of a small ruling élite, was assailed by a *laissez-faire* licence regulated only by the power of money. In the battle between the two, which nowhere in Scotland led to the outright victory of the latter on the scale to be found in the United States of America, capitalism nevertheless so far prevailed as to make the business of the High Street its own.

For retailing, with its dependence on a concentrated purchasing public to offset its considerable overheads and its corresponding need to be situated in the most accessible locations, has proved to be the aspect of the capitalist system which most needs the High Street. Cut-throat competition through price cutting (a favourite device of the multiples) has served only to reinforce the pressure for central location, so as to squeeze every last drop of potential custom from passers-by. Furthermore, because the landowners of the central area too have progressively adopted a similar ethic of market forces, land prices and rents have risen in response to demand, thus initiating a squeeze on retail profits and eliminating the least resourceful. Paradoxically, the area immediately surrounding what is known as the central business district is by contrast one of the least desirable (hence lowest-rated) areas of a town, as will be examined later in this chapter.

Historians have produced general models of the cost of central area rental per square foot in relation to the types of retail outlet which predominate. Highest land values are paid by the variety store, followed roughly in descending order by women's clothing, footwear, jewellery, furniture, men's clothing and grocery. Within each category, a common feature, even in very small towns, is clustering – the grouping together of shops of the same type within a particular area. Through time, the relative positions of the different categories can change, both in response to the circumstances of the town's inhabitants, and to the performance of the shops themselves, both locally and (for the multiples) in their national strategies. To give one example, the multiple food stores which originated in working-class areas moved into High Street locations in the inter-war years. By using valuation rolls, a local historian can easily trace these movements from the mid-nineteenth century and can follow through with a study of the shops' pricing and marketing strategies through the adverts in the local newspapers.

The architecture of the High Street has had a stormy history in the last 150 years. In many towns there was a 'rationalization' of the old market areas in the first half of the nineteenth century, with street widening, the demolition of old town ports and a relegation of traditional market functions to the covered market sidelines to make way for the first generation of permanent shops. In others a new shopping centre was created virtually from scratch, examples being Aberdeen's Union Street (where even the street itself was an artifice of engineering totally unrelated to contour) and Glasgow's Buchanan Street and Argyle Street axis. In Glasgow's case the old High Street was virtually abandoned and its buildings subsequently demolished such that it is difficult to envisage the street which bears that name today as the commercial and civic hub of the city two hundred years ago. Glasgow's is an extreme case of the shifting of the town centre by imperceptible degrees – again a phenomenon which can be studied through the rental values in valuation rolls. The shift usually appears to be westward – as with domestic suburbs west ends seem to be the most fashionable, though it is difficult to suggest a rational reason for this.

In most of Scotland's smaller towns, the relatively modest scale of economic development has meant the retention of the original central area, and in some cases much of the stone building from the first part of the nineteenth century. The persistence of the traditional land frontage measure of 18–21 feet (a secondary measure of 28 feet may represent a frontage plus side access) has helped to maintain this character. It is also often the case that though the façade of a shop, or more specifically the two metres at ground level above which nobody except local historians and architects look, may undergo dazzling but superficial alterations to accommodate every change of fashion and promotion of style, the rest of the building above stoutly retains its Victorian solidity or

Edwardian grace. Luckily, the penchant for High Street views among picture postcard manufacturers means that the local historian should be able to reconstruct changing shop frontages through the decades of this century.

There are towns in which more drastic alterations have occurred to a central area – redevelopment rather than abandonment. Dundee can serve as the examplar, having suffered transformation both by the Victorians, who nevertheless maintained a traditional curved building line, the characteristic stone and established height (that of the four-storey tenement); and from developers of the inter-war and post-1960 periods. In the latter town centre planning era, according to Naismith (1989), all was 'sacrificed in the interests of financial success'. The concrete pedestrianization which has resulted in many town centres has been much criticized, though perhaps it is too early to judge whether it will eventually acquire a period charm characterizing our own particular age.

Georgian and early nineteenth-century shops had often been formed from private houses, with little more alteration than modifications to the entrance door and a slight enlargement of the sash windows. Even the small panes (not very suitable for inspecting wares from the street) were often kept, despite the fact that even before the plate glass revolution of early Victorian times, glass sizes up to two feet three inches were available. It has been suggested that the retention of small panes (now often reintroduced to give a nostalgic effect) was a cheap imitation of fashionable bow windows, whose curved glass made small panes necessary. Small panes also had the practical advantage of being cheaper to replace after the attentions of vandals, seemingly as prevalent then as now.

The advent of plate glass led to the raising of lintels and the reduction of the stone frontage to a narrow band at ground level. To support the weight of the storeys above (three in the case of tenement shopping streets) stone pillars or mullions were required. Their vertical columns marched along most of Scotland's traditional High Streets and feature prominently in old picture postcards. Where local economies have been sluggish, they still survive in great numbers, enhancing the street with a sober and pleasing symmetry. Sometimes the pillars are simply carved, in other cases more intricately, with classical columns and other ornamentation. As Dean (1970) observes 'in shop architecture, as in exhibition architecture, there is a certain freedom from strict propriety. Both worlds are, or pretend to be, closer to the gaiety of make believe than to dull workaday fact. . . .' The high Victorian age brought more variants, for example arched windows instead of rectangular. The parades favoured by the Victorians embellished the fantasy further with graceful wrought iron ornamentation, whilst the Art Nouveau movement contributed its distinctive and popular spidery sinuosities, seen in carved doors, stained glass panels and signboards. The vogue for tiles has already been noted.

Plate glass, in conjunction with gas lighting, heralded the age of window display, previously considered vulgar. Attractive windows were part of a battery of marketing initiatives, which included sandwich boards, decorative billheads, advertisement hoardings and printed postcards of the premises, with the staff lined up for inspection. Many such items are familiar to users of local history library collections. A Lipton initiative, precursor of today's baking bread smell piped to the front of the supermarket, was to wedge coffee beans under entrance doors each morning.

Towards the end of the nineteenth century, architectural developments occurred which broke with the standard frontage known since Georgian times. The success of the co-operatives and department stores demanded new solutions to accommodate the larger scale of their operation and replace the irregular line of individual shop frontages which they had often taken over. The co-operatives sometimes favoured a style with baronial influences, often featuring a crest or inscription on a central gable, but all sorts of other styles have been used, much more widely in shops than in housing. The introduction of the steel beam allowed more extensive plate glass windows to be fitted, and the elimination of vertical stone columns. Department stores, under pressure in the highest land value areas and exploiting new inventions such as the lift (1850s) grew upwards as well as sideways to produce such glories as the Jenners building in Princes Street (described as Edwardian baroque) and the building at 80 George Street (now an exotic National Westminster Bank). Equally exuberant is Esslemont & Macintosh in Aberdeen's Union Street, summed up as 'part classical but loaded with Netherlandish detail' (Brogden, 1988).

The extensive plate glass of the department store can be considered appropriate in the context of the large city centre.

In smaller towns, it has often had a jarring effect, as for example in its adoption by the multiples, who in the inter-war years pursued a policy of standardizing their premises to promote a corporate image. Unfortunately, the materials used could be quite alien to the environment. Large plate glass frontages have also been the hallmark of supermarket development, which has had the most significant impact on High Street retailing in the post-war era.

The central business district and beyond

The model for the central business district posits three distinct zones, the inner retail (department stores, women's clothes), the outer retail (household and consumer goods) and the office area. The pattern can be roughly detected even in very small towns – Tivy (1961) cites the example of Aberfeldy in Perthshire (population 1,469 in 1981) centred on the town square.

If retailing dominates the core, commercial interests come second in the claim on central business district space. Lawyers and bankers have the longest pedigrees, and have tended to colonize those properties built as town mansions in the eighteenth and early nineteenth centuries by merchants moving out of crowded town centres into more airy and private locations. The attraction of these sites for the burgeoning banks of the nineteenth century (the period saw an explosive growth in national, provincial and local banks) was not unconnected with fostering an image of affluence as well as security. The deteriorating old town centres were bad for business. Edinburgh New Town's first arrival was the British Linen Bank in 1808, followed by the Royal Bank of Scotland, which took over the Dundas mansion house in St Andrew's Square in 1828. In Glasgow, five banks colonized Georgian houses in Virginia Street.

From the mid-nineteenth century the banks were no longer content to take over existing buildings, but pulled down the houses to build afresh. The banks themselves perhaps only occupied the ground floor, and let the upper storeys to valued customers such as solicitors at 'moderate rents to generate goodwill' says Checkland (1975). Valuation rolls will show the accuracy of the observation. The preferred architectural style for the purpose-built bank was Italian renaissance – 'prestigious and competitive' says Checkland, a symbol of security and authority with just a hint of Medici ruthlessness. Taylor (1973) sees connotations of efficiency, clarity, economy, civic administration and secular probity; and an advantage over the Italianate's main Victorian rival, Gothic, in that 'it was possible to conform to strict classical proportions without sacrificing much convenience'. This combination of semiotics and practicalities in the renaissance style led to its commercial adoption everywhere, despite what Taylor calls the 'haranguing of Gothic propagandists'. Only towards the end of the century did the French baroque Gothic, with its distinct ornate mansard windows and steep pitched roofs, muscle into town centres, though more often in the guise of the hotel or department store than the financial institution. Nineteenth-century hotels can dominate the main streets of resorts – Callander for example – featuring, in the words of McKean (1988) a variety of styles from 'patently fake nineteenth century black timber boarding' to 'banker's classical'.

A walk along Edinburgh's George Street will introduce one to the whole gamut of commercial architecture, and models for nearly all the buildings to be found in the smaller towns. The converted Dundas mansion has already been mentioned. Corinthian-columned frontages, inspired by the Greek revival of the early nineteenth century, feature on the Clydesdale Bank (Nos. 29–31) and the Royal Bank (No. 14). 'Yet another Temple to Mammon' is the description of McKean and Walker (1983), and Ruskin was equally caustic. 'How many Corinthian and Doric columns do you think there are in your banks and post offices, institutions, and I know not what else, one exactly like another?' he asked in despair. Edinburgh's main post office is in fact Italianate – the 'grandiose palazzo' on North Bridge corner, serving as a renaissance model for numerous small town post offices up and down the country with their typically neo-Georgian rusticated frontages. The high Italian style is followed on two of George Street's Bank of Scotland premises (at Nos. 62–6 and 101–3). In our own century, architectural adventurousness has been tempered by the need to balance the image of progressiveness with one of security. The Trustees Savings Bank at 28–30 Hanover Street is described by McKean and Walker as an 'unfriendly bank building in blank American style'. A more homely art deco was popular with many suburban and small town banks of the inter-war years, often single storey. Some High Street multiples also adopted the 'moderne' look, but the greatest enthusiasts for this were the cinemas. The survival of the rather stolid Victorian business centres in Scotland has been attributed to the depression which reduced demand for new development to a minimum.

The genesis of a modern style is linked to the growth of the office block. In the lettable block, each floor had to be of equal importance, a marketing consideration which was fundamentally at odds with the traditional classical hierarchy of smaller and simpler upper storeys. An early essay in alternative styles was Alexander 'Greek' Thomson's Egyptian Halls in Glasgow (1871–3) using the trabeated beam (construction based upon horizontal load-bearing) pioneered by the Prussian, Schinkel. Later, steel-framed buildings gave a new-found freedom from the load-bearing wall. The glass curtain made its debut between the wars, 'reappeared brilliantly at the Standard Life extension off George Street in the 1950s and then more controversially in Princes Street' suggest McKean and Walker (1983). Modern office building has been stimulated by the Offices, Shops and Railway Premises Act 1963 which made many structures obsolete through its insistence on higher standards of comfort and security. The blocks that have resulted have been much criticized. In the pursuit of maximum rental value, kit box architecture has been utilized, by developers and architects who may not even visit the town where their creations are to be realized. Functionalism without civic pride, and without even the necessity of the public appeal which must be taken into account by the image makers of retail architecture, can lead to a deadening dullness, though the local historian interested in pursuing this subject can remind himself or herself that town centre redevelopment led by local councils and planners has been as strongly disparaged. Any study of this topic will need to consider what the pressures are, on public and private bodies alike, which militate against architectural excellence.

The central business district rapidly gives way to a low status area, of warehouses, car salesrooms, parking and bus stations. Such an area can be identified even in very small Scottish burghs, where the workshops and small factories are often the successors of those which stretched along narrow burgage plots or along the rivers which provided the only source of power. Low status areas already existed in the medieval town – its inner fringe belt of ditches, water courses, back lanes (including the cowgates along which the burgesses' cattle were driven daily to pasture) and butts (where archery practice took place). Also extant in some old burghs are widened waste-ground areas just inside or outside the town gates where formerly there was grass and water for the horses that had brought produce to market. Appropriately enough, the area now sometimes sports the modern fuelling depot of a garage, a fate which also befell many of the old coaching inns which lost out to the railways. Railway companies built their own station hotels and drew others like a magnet in their direction.

The existence of the low status area in the modern town is explained by the principle that the use which can extract the greatest return from a given site will be successful in acquiring it. Highest potential return is from retailing, followed by commerce, industry/transportation, residences and finally agriculture. In the vicinity of the demarcation lines between one use and another are grey areas where it is uncertain what is the optimal use. For example, the advantage of a town centre location is the numbers of potential customers passing the door. For that advantage, high rents are paid. At the periphery of the shopping centre, however, there are slightly smaller concentrations of shoppers, so that the high turnover/high rent strategy becomes flawed.

For retailing, centrality has always been but one of many possible options, and high street growth over the last century has been paralleled by contrasting decentralizing pressures. An ancient and resilient craft is that of peddling, as far removed from the High Street idea as you can get. The traditional pedlar with his pack (or horse and cart when he became a little more prosperous) was joined in the nineteenth century by street sellers whose ranks were swelled during times of unemployment. Censuses reveal a truly dramatic increase in the number of itinerants, many of whom eked out a living with a miserable selection of wares or by acting as street salesmen to entice customers into shops. Registration (reinforced by the Pedlars Act 1870) attempted control, and registers of pedlars' certificates were kept by the police.

Pavement retailing existed in close symbiosis with suburban shopping centres, especially those for the working classes. The growth of towns beyond easy walking distance (and still without public transport) made suburban retailing a necessity, especially for perishables. Moreover, the central, fashionable shopping centres were quite deliberately made exclusive. 'The only working-class customers to cross their thresholds' says Davis (1966) 'were street hawkers coming to replenish their baskets and usually relegated to the side door'. The familiar shops of the working-class suburb included the second-hand clothes shop and the pawnbroker.

Middle-class suburbs eschewed the mêlée of shops found in the tenement blocks and single-storey lock-ups of working class areas, though where older villages were incorporated, the main street was usually transformed into a suburban centre. The antipathy to suburban shops also permeated the philosophy of the post-World War One council planners, who took similar exception to public houses (to this day they are rarely found on council estates). When suburban pubs were built 'they were often called hotels whether they took in guests or not, to preserve an air of respectability' (Barrett and Phillips, 1987). Fake medieval timbers and leaded windows were also favoured. Suburban shopping centres built in the 1930s and since often pay respect to Home Counties brick and concrete parades, with a whiff of the 'moderne'.

In the twentieth century street selling took on new dimensions, firstly with the door-to-door selling associated with electrical and cleaning goods (jokes about the salesmen reflecting the anxieties of trapped suburban housewives) and secondly with the introduction of the delivery van. Horses and carts had supplied a service in Victorian times, but the arrival of motor transport led to an enormous upsurge and trebled the area of a shop's operation. Co-operative societies ran fleets of vehicles – East Lothian for example had 50 vans in 1945 selling items as disparate as bread, milk, meat and groceries (this with wartime restrictions on van deliveries in force). More recently, the increase in car ownership, and altered work patterns for women, have been accompanied by a decline in this form of selling, though the same changes have thrown up a new rival to the high street – the cluster of hypermarkets on the outskirts of a town.

The growth of retailing from the seventeenth century was intricately linked to its obverse – an expansion of the equally reviled hoarding or wholesaling. Warehousing, closely associated with traditional ports and the activities of the merchant princes of the burghs, took on a new significance with large-scale food imports (grain and livestock initially). At the same time wholesale markets, taboo in the medieval economy, came to dominate the business of the traditional fairs, most of which adopted a specialist slant.

A century or two later, with the rise of the factory economy, armies of wholesale travellers (known as Manchester men) carried goods from textile and other factories along the roads that were rapidly replacing the coastal sea trading as the main avenue for distribution, sending many an old harbour town into decline and ensuring the survival, through lack of development pressure, of numerous eighteenth and early nineteenth century warehouses around its jetties.

A modern city or even a medium-sized town demanded more regular access to wholesale markets, particularly for food products, than could be afforded by a bi-annual fair. Urban wholesale markets often began life near railway termini, for obvious reasons, whilst regional centres such as Aberdeen provided the climate for the growth of auction marts (four in Aberdeen's case) which branched into the smaller agricultural towns. Road haulage developments of the inter-war years broke the interdependence of rail and market – farmers were aware that driving fat cattle on foot to the nearest railway station cost them half a hundred-weight per beast in weight. Market towns also saw the building of some fine corn exchanges and facilities for a variety of other wholesale markets – vegetables, agricultural machinery, nursery stock, feed stuffs and fertilizers. Suburban expansion has forced wholesale markets, by progressive steps, further and further from town centres to exploit cheap peripheral land. Here, 'they rub shoulders with the council-regulated abattoirs, banished on the grounds of amenity from the immediate vicinity of an increasingly squeamish populace' which has become divorced from rural realities. The global dimension of today's food industry is emphasized by Adams (1978) who sees the 'massive grain elevators' at Meadowside, Glasgow and Leith as 'symbols of the world of industry and trade' – cathedrals of commerce, just as factories and mills may be viewed as cathedrals of industry.

Urban industry

'Beginning with the rise of towns in the tenth and eleventh centuries' observes Olsen (1983), 'and enormously accelerated by the industrial revolution, some – eventually perhaps most – urban agglomerations came to have practical economic justification, producing more wealth than they consumed'. It was suggested at the start of this chapter that medieval towns flourished at the expense of the countryside. The other side of the coin is, firstly, the access to a range of goods not available from that same hinterland, and secondly the manufacturing capacity of the town itself, which takes advantage of the concentration of population that follows market concentration. Such an exploitation was slow to develop however – for instance, various large-scale and ambitious urban textile enterprises of the late seventeenth century failed.

For a period at the beginning of the Industrial Revolution, it appeared that industry and urbanization were not to proceed hand in hand, for dependence on raw materials such as coal, and water as a power source, gave industry little choice of location – hence sites such as New Lanark and Scotland's numerous mining villages. With improvements in steam power, however, the advantages of urban location became overwhelming, for the entrepreneurs, unmoved by the paternalistic impulses of a Robert Owen, could conveniently abdicate responsibility for their workforces' housing, health and education. The initial impetus to provide housing had waned, in the view of Doherty (1983), in the face of the 'decreasing need to attract labour with housing incentives as factory disciplines became more widely accepted and tolerated'. Non-involvement could also be justified in that it allowed families whose members were employed at different factories to find the 'optimum' location for their residence. A noticeable feature of the Scottish economy has been the complete divorce of industrial and housing capital; and the economic history of towns over the last century and a half has revolved around tensions between local authorities and business interests, and between fostering the precious resource of people and their well-being (in housing and services), and the taxation of business to pay for that well-being. An average of one third of a town's workforce is employed in industry, and ten per cent of its surface area given over to industrial production, so a fine tuning in the balance is absolutely essential to ensure the prosperity of the local community.

Reference has already been made to the fluctuating boundaries between retailing and manufacturing, merchants and craftsmen, in medieval towns. Guild and incorporation records – of merchants and craftsmen respectively – do not survive before the sixteenth century, which means that archaeology must be used to study early industrial production. Spearman (1988) confirms the close relationship between manufacturing and the farming cycle, for both labour and materials: 'one craftsman's waste produce was more often than not another's raw material. Hence cattle slaughtered in towns became the raw material not only of fleshers, but tanners, cordwainers, cobblers, bone workers (making pins, needles, dice, knife handles, bobbins and toggles), rope-makers, horners, gutters, candlemakers and others'. The triple access to materials, markets and skills set the town apart from the countryside, and heralded the symbiosis of industry and urbanism. Location was in workshops attached to the craftsmen's/retailers' homes, for such was the integration of manufacturing and retailing that industrial zones as we know them hardly existed, though skinners' and tanners' yards were situated away from town centres because of their unpleasant smells. Even in industrial towns of the nineteenth century, high street sites for manufacturing are not unknown. In Prestonpans near Edinburgh, for example, soapworks and saltpans were operating in the central shopping area.

The advantage of urban location even provided a magnet for agriculturally-based industrial processes such as grain processing and wool milling, away from their source of raw materials. Favoured sites were the banks of rivers and canals outside the traditional town limits, where there was space for the complex and militarily precise sequence of operations that constituted the new factory economy. Linear concentration along the lengths of the rivers followed. Just as these mills took over the sites of small-scale grain mills, so they in turn have often given way to other industrial uses no longer dependent on water power.

For a town that prospered, the original green field sites gradually became more and more central until, towards the end of the Victorian period, various factors led to changes in location. The new larger-scale production units could not be accommodated in congested central sites, whilst improving rail links and the introduction of tram and motor transport made a peripheral site away from river and canal systems feasible, both for workforce access and for the supply and distribution of materials. The availability of electrical power also freed industry from reliance on coal deliveries. Heavy industry gravitated to large, railway linked sites often located near water supplies. Port-based industries moved down river, leading to the meteoric rise of towns such as Clydebank and

Methil. Light industry moved towards environmentally attractive suburban locations, becoming associated with zonal planning concepts in which a town for the first time was conceived in terms of segregated functions – production, retailing, residential. The pioneer industrial estate, pioneering also in its adoption of public sponsorship for business development, was Hillington (Glasgow) and the Scottish Industrial Estates Corporation opened three others on the edge of the city by 1939. The idea was soon copied, for example by Aberdeen's Kincorth, more ambitious in the planning than the execution.

There are many exceptions to these rules of industrial decentralization, notably the persistence of the 'inner city' manufacturing district in towns suffering from a stagnant economy. The striking central appearance of Galashiels, dominated by its mills, is a case in point. The pattern among such burghs, whose origin is as marketing and industrial centres for an agricultural hinterland and whose growth has been fitful or non-existent, is of the persistence in fairly central locations of long established enterprises. Distilleries and mills have been mentioned – one can add those industries which maintain medieval craft skills, such as bakeries and meat curers, and more recent craft skills such as printing (for which there is a particular logic in a central location to service the surrounding business area). The long surviving lemonade factory in Dingwall (established in 1890) is one of the many once operating from high street chemists. Even in these small towns, however, it is interesting that the same forces are operating to shift production to the periphery, either to new factory units provided by the state or local council, or to sites chosen by the businesses themselves on economic grounds.

The concept of government intervention in the urban market place has become more widely accepted. The provision of subsidy on Clydeside under the Special Areas (Development and Improvement) Act of 1934 was extended under the Distribution of Industry Act 1945 to include many other regions. The development districts of 1960 changed the emphasis to more restricted areas subject to high levels of unemployment, a policy reversed within a few years with the adoption of extensive development areas and special development areas. The philosophy of the 1980s has introduced the enterprise zones, a reversion to the small-scale approach, and has been inspired by a deregulating rather than subsidizing ethos. It would be interesting for a local historian to consider various industrial projects in his or her town that reflect the changing approach of government over these 60 years, not only to compare the reality with the hopes, but to assess the extent to which planning can in the long run determine the economic welfare of a town. A twentieth-century feature to be taken into account is that capital for industrial investment comes not from the locality, but from financial and manufacturing companies from outside, looking for a good return on investment. As Checkland (1976) notes: 'such a pattern commits the receiving region to the broader strategy of multinational businesses, which by their nature compare the relative returns to investment in various countries and act accordingly'. Several Scottish towns have learned this to their cost in recent years; and the point illustrates the impossibility of a local historian adopting a parochial approach to his or her subject. Indeed the very concept of a discrete town is questionable in an economically fluid society with transport networks which begin to undermine the centuries-old rationale for having concentrations of population at all.

'Capital', claimed Lewis Mumford (1966) 'tended to favour buildings of a utilitarian character, quick to construct, easy to replace – except when the need for public confidence in an institution's wealth and solidity justified a heavy investment in ostentatious masonry'. Plain utilitarianism, particularly in association with the simple principles of classical harmony, is today often seen as a virtue, its restraint contrasting with the eclectic extravagance found elsewhere in towns. Praised examples are Dens Mill in Dundee and the Ferguslie Mills built for Coats in the 1880s and now mainly demolished. Their renaissance inspiration has led to their being considered 'the most magnificent cotton mills in Scotland'. 'Judicious use of Classic or Egyptian details' has also been noted in the design of factory entrance gates, chimneys and engine houses (Jones, 1968); and Millman (1975) draws attention to the 'whimsical nuances of "industrial baronial" '. In the inter-war years, the streamlined ocean liner style of avant-garde European architects was sometimes enthusiastically adopted, its functionalism proving more attractive in the industrial setting than for domestic housing. Modern industry too has adopted the contemporary, in the form of what Brogden (1988) calls 'brightly coloured warehouses with improbable names'. Brogden has praise for Donside House in Ellon Road,

Aberdeen which 'shows how attention to detail and composition lifts a shed warehouse out of the ordinary'.

Research ideas and sources

Documentation of the history of enterprises is helped by mid-nineteenth-century legislation which introduced the limited liability company. Limited liability was generally considered a long overdue measure, the absence of which had retarded economic growth and risk-taking by entrepreneurs. This liberalization was protected by a system of registration, with the company registration office in George Street, Edinburgh, where each company was obliged to deposit share prospectuses, names of shareholders, proposed new share issues and annual reports. Records of defunct businesses are passed to West Register House in Charlotte Square.

The number of companies incorporated was considerable, nearly 3,000 by the end of the century. Most remained very small, with an average life of under 20 years. The numbers involved in public utilities (which tended to have longer lives of around 35 years) almost matched those in manufacturing. Much of the shareholding remained locally based, as the list of shareholders' names and addresses will show, a state of affairs encouraged by the continuing existence of local stock exchanges in Scottish cities. The rapport of such businesses with their local community will surely, on investigation, prove to be a different kind of relationship from that of multinational exploiting local opportunity noted above.

The paucity of information about the numerous small breweries, gas works, retail and financial service companies is unfortunate, and official company registers may do little more than identify the fact of their existence. The obvious directories, valuation rolls, maps, newspapers and other sources mentioned in previous chapters are equally applicable to studies of businesses, and can be supplemented by miscellanies of trade catalogues and other ephemera found in local history libraries and museums. There is no substitute for visual evidence, and the National Monuments Record has some fine studies of buildings and machinery, recently supplemented by the transfer to it of the records of the Scottish Industrial Archaeology Survey, formerly held by Strathclyde University. The camaraderie of shared work is captured in reminiscence collections and workplace photographs in

PROSPECTUS

OF THE

PRESTONPANS GAS COMPANY.

In consequence of a very general desire having been expressed by the inhabitants of Prestonpans to avail themselves of the bene-fit of Gas-light, preliminary arrangements have been made by a provisional committee for forming a Company with the object of lighting the town and so much of the neighbourhood, as may be deemed desirable, with Gas.

When the situation of inland towns and villages, where gas is profitably manufactured, notwithstanding of a carriage of from 30s. to 20s. per ton upon the coal, is taken into consideration, it is obvious that Prestonpans, situated in a Coalfield, has infinite advantages over these in point of locality. Cheapness of material, with the probability of a large consumpt, promises for the above undertaking a good return for the capital invested.

Besides shops and dwelling-houses in the main street of Prestonpans, there are several factories where a considerable consumpt of gas will take place, viz. a Distillery, Brewery and Malting, a Soapwork, Saltwork and Pottery, the proprietors of which take a deep interest in the success of the undertaking.

An eligible site has already been obtained for the erection of the buildings, the ground has been surveyed, and the plans and specifications are in rapid progress; it is therefore expected that the works may be in operation within a few months.

The Capital to be £.1000, divided into two hundred Shares of £.5 each. £.1 per share to be paid as a deposit on allocation of the shares.

The Company to be constituted when one-half of the Capital Stock is subscribed for.

The management to be vested in Directors to be appointed by the Company.

Application for Shares may be made to Messrs ROBERT HISLOP, WILLIAM ALEXANDER, ALEX KNOX, JOSEPH DRYSDALE & J. MELLIS, all in Prestonpans, who will furnish the printed forms.

As the Shares are nearly all subscribed for, the Lists will be closed on 21st September, that being the last day on which applications will be received.

JAMES MELLIS, Interim Sect.

Prestonpans 8th Sept. 1845.

J. WALKER, PRINTER, MUSSELBURGH.

A share prospectus of the kind commonly found in the records of registered companies held in West Register House and (for those still extant) by the Registrar of Companies. Small, locally-based enterprises proliferated in Victorian towns, after limited liability legislation protected the promoters from loss of their personal assets in the event of bankruptcy.

private, company and local history library archives. Company records have been surveyed by the Business Archives Council and by the National Register of Archives, administered through Glasgow University Archives and the Scottish Record Office respectively, both of whom have substantial archives of business papers themselves. Sequestration and bankruptcy records are held in West Register House, and the official listing of bankruptcies is given in the *Edinburgh Gazette*.

Industrial archaeology involves research techniques which a competent amateur can successfully pursue when faced with a dearth of information from other sources. Measured drawings of industrial sites require little in the way of equipment apart from a long measuring tape (preferably 100 feet). As many measurements as possible should be made from a single fixed point to minimize the effect of any errors. Inside buildings, floor areas should be measured across diagonals as well as along walls so that the shape of the space can be accurately plotted even when angles are not square. Any surviving machinery and its position should be carefully recorded. In drawing and in compiling an accompanying photographic record, an effort should be made to identify the operational flow, from receipt of materials to dispatch of the finished product, in other words the logic of the layout. Industrial archaeologists are often asked to date buildings, where documentary and map evidence is lacking. Major (1975) gives some key indicators. For example 'patent fire proof construction of cast-iron columns and beams supporting brick-arch floors cannot have been built before the 1790s'. He adds, however, that they continued in use for a hundred years. Similarly, cast iron windows span the period from 1800 to the introduction of the galvanized mild-steel window in this century.

Cross sections of the business activity of a burgh at intervals of a decade can include employment in different sectors, a summary of retailing outlets, and location charts of industrial sites. Alternatively the history of a single site can be plotted over the last century.

Processes can be studied too – how the delivery of produce was organized or how a strategy of expansion was carried out by a specific firm. The relationship between a business and the town to which it belongs can be interesting, not just its political relationship with the local council but the provision of housing and social and cultural facilities for its workers and others, its sponsorship of local events. This all contributes to the cultivation of what today we would call its profile.

Chapter Five

THE PUBLIC TOWN

In 1862 North Berwick Town Council received a bill of five pounds, for one hogshead of ale to celebrate the wedding of the Prince of Wales. The period was a watershed for the old town councils whose corruption, dating from a 1469 act of parliament establishing self-perpetuating oligarchies, is no more strongly exemplified than in Forfar, where, in 1803, a boy of 12 was appointed town clerk; in 1822 he was shown to be mentally handicapped, but could not be dismissed as he had been appointed for life. The 'inn parlour, club room manner of the old civic life' (as Martin, 1968 calls it), where burgesses 'grazed their cattle on the common land, and occasionally, if there was a dividend to be disposed of, had a modest treat' was about to be swept away in the larger towns; and with it the cosy parlour of the burgh chambers. We move, says Martin, into 'the chill, impersonal world of the ruled-feint ledger: the buildings themselves say so'.

New buildings often meant new sites. Burgh chambers, tolbooths and townhouses (the variant names indicating the multiple uses of the town's only public building) had been strategically placed in the High Street, but lost out to commercial interests. Paradoxically, their original prominent position was itself a compromise with private interests. For where the tolbooth had an island site (as in Dumfries) it was owing to the private ownership of High Street burgage plots, so that public buildings, when first conceived in the late middle ages, had to be built in the free public space of the street. In some cases, subsequent market area colonization has made the town house part of an island 'mid row'. Another solution was to build the tollbooth jutting out from the main street into the market area.

If the most prestigious sites were sometimes lost in the new nineteenth-century towns, compensation could be sought in architectural extravagance. Of the craggy baronial general post office in Crown Street, Aberdeen (1907) Brogden (1988) says 'it calls attention to itself as a public building should' and this philosophy was endorsed by many town hall builders, no more so than by those of Greenock. With the Victoria Tower of almost 250 feet dominating the town, the Municipal Buildings testify to its nineteenth-century wealth with 'a complex design drenched in classical detail and sculpture, with lavishly garnished interiors' (Walker, 1986). One shipowner, less impressed, opined in 1888 that 'every beauty but the beauty of economy has been studied in the erection of the Municipal Buildings'. Hostility to the civic grandeur of what has been called 'the local state' was also felt by the working classes, who found the new town hall 'undoubtedly magnificent but on land gained at the cost of clearing the homes of the poor' (Fraser, 1985). Aberdeen's townhouse of 1872 was built at the expense of Huxter Row, one of the city's oldest streets. When eviction notices were served on the tenants, one petitioned the council, with intended or unintended irony, to allow the removal of 'the almost indispensible comodit, my water closet' which 'would be of little value to the said gentlemen and might be very useful to me' (quoted in Wyness, 1971).

Eighteenth- and early nineteenth-century rebuilding favoured the Georgian style, but the Victorians demanded greater rhetoric. The adoption of Scots baronial led for the rest of the century (notes Walker, 1985) to 'variants of the tower, spire-topped, with gablet or dormer sandwiched between conically-roofed corbelled corner turrets'. Riotous contributions from French and Flemish baroque-gothic adorn the more florid, as in Dunfermline. Some burghs could have two stabs at rebuilding, a notorious example being Dundee, which demolished a fine William Adam edifice in favour of the current Roman senate. The more intelligent Inverness solution was to build a baronial gothic town hall across the street from its eighteenth-century forebear. The small police burgh foundations of the nineteenth century could not afford any of these extravagances, and had to be content with plain Italianate or even a humble office in a main street terrace. Premises were sometimes shared with the various other local authorities which emerged in the nineteenth century, such as parish councils.

The modest Dutch-style tolbooths of the sixteenth and seventeenth centuries, and to some extent their Georgian descendants, are multi-purpose buildings, incorporating council chamber, market office, strongroom and bank, court-room, police station and gaol. They were also the showpiece for the council's investment in modern technology – the clock. Tollbooth cells continued to be used as local prisons during the nineteenth century, but for serious offenders these were supplanted by large purpose-built gaols following the Prisons Act of 1839. As much as thirty years before, Aberdeen had pioneered the building of a bridewell for petty offenders. Keith (1972) reflects that 'with its imposing entrance from Union Street, its elegant gateway, porter's lodge and guard-house and its 14-foot wall enclosing a garden and exercise grounds, it was perhaps the first example in Aberdeen of the extravagant elaboration in rate-supported institutions which is today's commonplace'.

Law enforcement in one form or another was behind much nineteenth-century public building. The Sheriff Court Houses (Scotland) Act 1860 led to the construction of numerous sheriff courts in the following decades, financed 50 per cent by the central government treasury and under the supervision of the commissioners of supply, the group of local aristocrats who performed many of the functions later undertaken by county councils after their foundation in 1889. The commis-sioners often merged their different responsibilities in groups of buildings incorporating county offices and courts. Fittingly, for edifices representing Scotland's independent legal tradition, most were baronial in style, famous examples being David Rhind's at Dumfries (1863–6) and Selkirk (1870) and Peddie and Kinnear's at Greenock (1887) and Aberdeen (1868–74). Police stations were another category of building that became differentiated from the tolbooth, the 1857 Police (Scotland) Act sanctioning the building of 'station houses and strong rooms or lock-ups'.

The appearance of barracks in nineteenth-century towns brings a wheel full circle, for the original head or caput of a burgh had usually been a military institution – the lord's or king's castle where the functions of meeting place and court, later transferred to the town's own tolbooth, had been executed. Barracks supplanted billeting, for, as Brice (1984) explains: 'Railways and steamships meant that the opening phase of a war could develop very quickly. Time could be wasted contacting and rounding up troops scattered about in billets or half-ruined castles. Modern armies needed to be concentrated in areas where they could undertake indoor and outdoor training programmes and yet still be ready to proceed overseas at the shortest notice.' Rows of wooden huts or barrack blocks were the result, supplemented by drill halls in most towns, where reservists and volunteers could also be trained in the use of weapons of growing sophistication.

Middle-class professionals and civic pride

Civic consciousness – the recognition of the public character of towns – has been a movement cultivated by the professional classes. They were, for example, responsible for the conservation philosophy which arose in the early nineteenth century, with some often injudicious restoration of old buildings; and it was they who first held up to a town's gaze the mirror of its own history, through the antiquarian society, the reprinting of old records, the museum and the revival of long dead architectural styles.

The professional classes formed a small but influential group within the bourgeoisie of the eighteenth and nineteenth centuries. It has been estimated (Nenadic, 1988) that they constituted about ten per cent of the total, though up to 20 per cent in the professionally-dominated Edinburgh and as little as five per cent in the very small towns. The main components were the legal profession (initially linked closely to landed interests), churchmen, university and school teachers, the military, and the scientific fraternity, medical men especially.

Given the relative openness of Scotland's educational system, these professionals were produced in far greater numbers than were demanded by native society and industry. Consequently, their talents were exported world-wide through, for instance, the colonial and armed services. Such men often returned to their homeland to retire, injecting their wealth into the local economy together with their acquired taste for exotic artefacts and furnishings. The public memorials which they erected or which were erected in their memory in so many towns are often influenced stylistically by such models. Generally, public statues and monuments (whose complex intentions are worth a study in themselves) typify the educational and civic values of the professional classes.

On a wider scale, one can sense the professional contributions to the tone and style of towns such as Edinburgh and Perth. Their 'polite' society shared an outlook which Nenadic (1988) describes as 'an emphasis on intellectual improvement, rational enquiry and the positive use of time' – values reflected

in the genteel townscapes which they inspired. These townscapes will perhaps also reveal to the investigator the influence
of the professionals' strong democratic instincts, in, for
example, the use of open space.

The specific institutions promoted by the class were already
burgeoning in the eighteenth century, particularly in
Edinburgh. Dumfries, in the statistical account of 1791, is
described as having 'become remarkable as a provincial town
for elegance, information and varied amusements'; and in the
next generation or two many towns acquired a literary club or
magazine, a scientific society, a theatre and a local newspaper.
The Scottish scientific intellect, led by the statisticians, was
also brought to bear on urban problems, with promotion of
the leafy suburb, the subscription hospital and numerous
philanthropic societies (regarded by some historians as
mechanisms to control the urban poor). The industrial town
apart, professional concerns permeate the development of the
nineteenth-century urban landscape, and indeed have continued to do so.

Local government

It is no exaggeration to say that the debate over sanitation was
the dominant preoccupation of industrial towns for at least the
first half-century of their existence. Social welfare came a very
poor second in the minds of local councils, and the provision
of educational or recreational facilities an even poorer third.
Indeed, when the latter did move into the forefront of debate
at the end of the nineteenth century, there were many voices
raised in defence of the 'ratepayer' which argued that libraries,
museums and gardens were entirely outside the remit of local
government.

The case for sanitation at public expense was not easily
accepted. The most telling argument in the long run was one
of social engineering, for it was realized that sanitary improvements would help to provide a healthy and contented workforce. A disciplined and concentrated pool of labour was the
sine qua non of large-scale industrial society, and with limited
transport this population had to be closely regimented.

Of course, the middle classes who led the industrial
revolution found sanitation desirable for themselves also, and
they immediately used their newly won political franchise of
the 1830s to promote a series of police acts (1833, 1847, 1850

and 1862). These gave powers to public meetings convened at the behest of as few as seven of their number, to set up local authorities to oversee cleansing, water supply, lighting and paving. Policing in nineteenth-century terminology refers to these functions, not the more restricted function we now assign to it. Of the 200 or so burghs which existed at the end of the nineteenth century, around half were police burghs established under these acts. Royal burghs and burghs of barony were the first to benefit from the legislation (1833) with a resulting dual administration of traditional magistrates and new police commissioners. The 1847 act allowed police functions to be completely absorbed. The 1850 and 1862 acts introduced a new category of police burghs in urban areas previously without any form of government. The formation of other *ad hoc* authorities followed, for poor relief (parochial boards from 1845) and schooling (school boards from 1872). Only with reluctance was the concept of an all-embracing local authority accepted towards the end of the century (county councils 1889, town councils 1892 and 1900) for such local concentration of power was at odds with a belief in free-market economics. It is interesting to see in the last few years a revival of the local government *ad hoc* philosophy (with for instance regenerated school boards) under the impetus of a similar market ethos. As in the nineteenth century, this devolution of power in the name of democratic rights can be interpreted as an attempt to stifle local autonomy by division, whilst giving space to the more affluent to cultivate a narrow class-based garden; or alternatively, as a reaffirmation of individual endeavour. Perhaps the most important question for the local historian is whether the dismantling of local power structures leads to the evaporation of that power, which is thus proved to be arbitrarily repressive, or whether in fact it constitutes a subtle and surreptitious transfer of the same powers to private interests. In essence the question is this: would our towns look any different if the controls that have been imposed had not existed? A local historian can make a judgement through a study of local authority objectives and achievements over the last century.

The antithesis of the *ad hoc* philosophy was also a nineteenth-century invention – the so-called municipal socialism pioneered by Glasgow Town Council. It viewed the town more as a coherent organism in which individual interests must be subject to the organism's controlling authority, the council. Glasgow's socialism was engendered by crisis, blossomed in civic aspiration, and reached its climax in direct management of the city's economy, causing it to be labelled in as sober a publication as the *Scottish Law Review* in 1905 as 'the oppressor of the west'. The term 'municipal socialism' is somewhat misleading – the 'oppressor of the west' is more accurately described by Checkland (1976) as 'a joint-stock company run by the middle classes', a far cry from the Labour-controlled council (post-1933) which saw itself as a 'social service . . . centred upon public sector housing at low rents'. At that time the council's control of building sites drove virtually all private building firms from the city.

The municipal movement began with a sanitation and housing crisis highlighted by the introduction of civil registration of births, marriages and deaths in 1855. The battle for the water supply from Loch Katrine was won with the inauguration in 1859, a medical officer of health was appointed in 1862 and the City Improvement Act of 1866 led to a vigorous programme of slum clearance (the first in the United Kingdom). The years 1870–90 saw the rise of municipal trading, beginning with gas municipalization in 1869. Parliament was opposed to direct local authority operation of the then new tramways, but Glasgow won the case for ownership of the tramlines which ran through its streets. These it leased to private operators, stipulating fare levels in the contracts. Full municipalization followed in 1894. Economic control reached its zenith with successful municipal banks established in Kirkintilloch, Irvine, Clydebank and Motherwell. Museums, galleries, golf courses, tennis courts, bowling greens, telephones and libraries kept Glasgow in the forefront. By 1902, according to C. M. Allan (quoted in Best, 1968) the corporation owned, among other properties, '2,488 houses, 78 lodging houses, 372 shops, 86 warehouses and workshops, 12 halls, 2 churches and a bakehouse'.

Glasgow's expenditure on public building projects between 1873 and 1914 averaged about one third of that spent on house building, the cycle in public works tending to follow the boom and slump of the private market. During the peak years of the 1890s, major projects were undertaken by many councils. Hawick and Paisley spent £2,500 and £8,000 respectively on swimming baths, and Coatbridge £10,000 on a library. Dumbarton council was 'heavily involved in schemes connected with the pier, gasworks, water mains, roads and footpaths, layout of cemeteries and parks and planning a town hall' (Rodger, 1975). The inauguration of public contracts in Dunfermline in 1913, valued at more than was spent that year on the entire housebuilding programme, could not but have a large influence on the level of the latter as well as on industrial investment. The local historian can observe similar patterns in Falkirk (1909–12), and in Coatbridge throughout the Edwardian period (with a colossal valuation of public work by 1912 at over five times that spent on house building).

Hostility to municipal socialism came from various quarters. Most of the middle classes were reluctant to credit local government with any role beyond that of responding 'to the local economy, to run selected services effectively and to keep local taxes at a reasonable level. Once an economy showed signs of weakening, the gloss could soon disappear from civic enterprise' (Hart, 1982). Indeed, many middle-class groups opted out of civic oneupmanship altogether by exploiting a loophole in the police acts, to establish what were basically suburbs as independent burghs (areas such as Crosshill, Govanhill, Hillhead and Pollokshields East and West in Glasgow). These suburbs pursued the same self-interest in exclusivity as the supporters of the *ad hoc* philosophy noted above. Hostility also emanated from the proletariat, who appear to have regarded the local state in terms of raids on ticketed lodging houses, clearance of one's family's homes, means-tested parochial boards, and insolent and interfering police – feelings liberally laced with scorn for civic extravagance and contempt for the salaries of its underworked minions. Not only were many of the working class disenfranchised, those who did have a vote lost the privilege if rates had not been paid in full before the elections. More than one quarter of Glasgow households were excluded in the 1890s. The local historian can trace the persistence and assess the justice of these different attitudes up to the present day.

The researcher will likely find little sign of the ferment of municipal socialism and its descendants in a study of Scotland's small burghs. Far from owning a differentiated collection of public buildings, the town clerk often doubled as a local solicitor with his offices in the council chambers, and the behaviour of the councillors maintained something of the tradition of the inn parlour councils with which this chapter began. Their lack of pretension perhaps helped their resilience,

THE Musselburgh Sporting Chronicle.

MONDAY, 4th NOVEMBER 1889.

NOTES ON THE MUSSELBURGH PLATE

BY OUR "PRIVATE CORRESPONDENT."

CORRECT LIST O' STARTERS AND JOCKEYS.

HORSES.	COLOURS.	RIDERS.
1. Grey horse, "Auctioneer," *ly "Unquebagh" out of "Restaurant," by "The Vandal" —"Destruction," aged	Funeral black Lincoln green belt, piebald cap.	J. Jones.
2. Roan horse, "Fawkie Willis" by "Mainchatoe" out of Number "One," 6 years	Venetian red, turpentine hoops, red cap.	R. Drybone jun.
3. Black colt," "Chloroform †" by "Stable Boy" out of Lady Love," 4 years	Lavender, rose sleeves, black cap.	A.W. Leather
4. Chestnut horse, "Verbosity ‡" by "Old Lead" out of "Windbag" by "Free Kirk"—"Vanity," 6 years	Gordon tartan, lead belt and cap.	G. Aiken.
5. Black horse, "Peter Biot" by Makeshift" out of "Confusion" 5 years	White, black spots and cap.	Adams, jun.
6. Brown colt, "Scrapecaulk" by "Old Musselburgh," out of "Erin-go-Bragh, 3 years	Brick red, Irish green sleeves and cap.	J. Robinson.
7. Bay horse, "Double Shuffle," by "Hesitancy" out of "Inconsistency" out of "Loretto," 4 years	Beetroot, yellow stripes and cap.	J. Johnson.
8. Black colt, by "Old Tory" out of "Loretto," 4 years	Scarlet and white.	J. Plasterer.

* This horse will be sold without reserve to dissolve a partnership immediately after the race—not warranted free from vice, but a sure foal-getter

† This horse is also for sale, but in the private sale list. Reserve price, 1000 guineas, would make a valuable stud horse.

‡ This horse has been disposed of to the Whisky Ring Syndicate, and will run

well as his wind is simply inexhaustible. His action is decidedly free and he is strongly supported by the whisky syndicate. Lush goes a long way nowadays. His trainer, Captain Bung, has great faith in it. I fear Verbosity's soft spot will show at the finish, and he will just miss the place for which he is backed, as big Georgie is so featherweight.

Peter Biot, late "Evening News," is still rickety on the legs, but has slightly improved in appearance and public estimation since his failure in last year's race. He is evidently at his best just now and, as the sandy ground at the back of the course seems to suit his peculiar swagger, he may scramble into a place. At one time it was likely that the temperance house jockey, Tommy Dundee, would be in the saddle, but negotiations having failed, I understand that the crack light-weight, Adams jun., has been specially retained, and if he can only keep the old horse's head straight he may win a place, but I fear that he will have a difficult task, as the son of Makeshift and Confusion is generally all over the field at the finish.

Double Shuffle, late "13 Bob." This old horse is looking remarkably fresh and well after his twelve months' rest. He is big and strong enough, but generally shows the white feather when the finish comes. His old jockey, Jimmy Johnston, will ride him as usual, and as he has him under his private care at "Babby's," he ought to be able to give a good account of him. The rider has been put upon a rigid T.T. diet to reduce his weight and steady his nerves. The Whisky Ring are laying heavily against this horse—the Commissioner—Big Harry—usually identified with the syndicate, laying 10 to 1 in monies against him the other day. I trust he will improve upon last year's appearance when he was broken out of place by the cart horse Rob Roy by *long head.*

Loretto Colt.—This long kept good thing is actually entered at last, but is many other good things I fear he has been spoilt in the keeping. He is no public form to go by, but his private trials have evidently pleased his ty, who will do their best for him as they always do even when it is hopely. This colt is a regular dark one, and I know nothing about him, and can

A section from a popular form of Victorian electioneering spoof, with comments on the candidates for a Musselburgh town council election 1889. The vituperative style, with talk elsewhere of 'cripples' and 'thickness in the head' is perhaps a symptom of enthusiasm for the infant democracy.

for they survived two major restructurings of local government up to their much lamented demise in 1975.

The uniform burghs that resulted from the acts of 1892 and
1900 (the term 'police burgh' became obsolete, and commissioners became councillors) still left education and poor relief
in the hands of *ad hoc* bodies, though democratic parish
councils replaced parochial boards in 1894 and county-wide
educational authorities supplanted the myriad school boards
in 1918. The debate leading up to the major local government
reform of 1929 addressed the question of the integral relationship between a town and its hinterland, with proposals for
broader local authorities. The cities had already absorbed most
of their rebellious independent suburbs, but in the event, the
act failed to dislodge the intransigent independence of the
other small burghs. The involved compromise gave the four
major cities of Aberdeen, Dundee, Edinburgh and Glasgow
county status, with all the powers of a county council. A
limited number of towns with populations over 20,000
became 'large burghs' with relatively wide powers (for town
planning, highways and some aspects of public health) leaving
'small burghs' with a rump of responsibilities for housing,
building control, refuse collection and the like. This situation
remained basically unaltered until 1974, with the county
councils and their satellite district councils co-operating with
town councils on an array of joint boards and committees.

Town planning

'Without design' was a laudatory term in the Victorian period,
claims Mumford (1966). If this is so the Housing, Town
Planning etc Act of 1909 heralded a new age, in which local
councils began to lay claim to the ordering of their towns'
space.

Amongst all the piecemeal development of local government in the nineteenth century, the idea that it should take
responsibility for the physical space of the town was one of the
slowest to gain a foothold. The Land Clauses Act of 1845
facilitated compulsory purchase, escaping the fate of the early
working-class housing acts (the Torrens acts of 1868, 1879 and
1882) – that of being virtually inapplicable to Scotland because
of differences in law. The pragmatism of nineteenth-century
legislation was firmly directed towards demolition; the 1909
act introduced planning as a positive concept. It stipulated that

a town planning scheme might be imposed over any area of land which was being or seemed likely to be developed. The councils' remit was restricted to a consideration of the needs for sanitation, amenity and convenience. Town authorities were not envisaged as the ultimate arbiters however, as the Local Government Board reserved for itself the judgment as to whether a proposed scheme was warranted in each situation as it arose.

The planning authorities which emerged from the Town and Country Planning (Scotland) Act 1932 were the county councils and the councils of large burghs (plus two small burgh exceptions). There followed the Restriction of Ribbon Development Act 1935 which stretched the authorities' powers into the countryside, where a mushroom growth of bungalows, petrol stations and advertisement hoardings had occurred. The 1943 Town and Country Planning (Interim Development (Scotland)) Act finally brought all land under a local government regulatory umbrella. The innovatory nature of the reports which inspired these statutes has been contrasted with the great nineteenth-century town reports highlighting poverty and problems of poor public health. Preoccupation with 'social issues . . . the pressures of capital . . . or agricultural decline' is replaced by a 'novel aesthetic focus' (King, 1984).

For the local historian, one important significance of the 1947 Town and Country Planning (Scotland) Act was the obligation on planning authorities to prepare development plans by June 1951, and thereafter to revise and update them periodically. The research or survey data contained in these plans and their successors are an important study source. Another provision of the act was the designation of comprehensive development areas for town centres; and by 1964 one third of all urban local authorities in the United Kingdom had drawn up redevelopment proposals which often resulted in the clearing away of a traditional centre. In Glasgow, for example, Worsdall (1979) felt that 'the designation of an area for comprehensive development in fact gave the local authority the totally unnecessary and grossly abused power of wholesale demolition, and its application . . . has resulted in the systematic and wanton destruction of much that was finest in the city's architecture'. It has been said that 'a city without old buildings is like a man without a memory' (quoted in Ward, 1968), yet the demolitions of the 1960s are but the latest manifestation of a long tradition – even recently, in the 1930s, whole quarters of what we would now regard as charming examples of the vernacular were swept away. An economic view of the matter is that a town's retention of old buildings is in inverse proportion to its success, and those marvellous preservations in aspic such as the seventeenth-century town of Culross are so preserved precisely because they have failed as towns. This and the demolition ethos of Victorian legislation appear to have been as influential in the deliberations of local authorities as the aesthetic ideals of planners, though a study of local council minute books over the last century will give the most accurate picture for any particular town. Town centres which have been extensively redeveloped include Greenock, Inverness and Clydebank. The most recent have been heavily influenced by ideas of pedestrian/vehicular segregation pro-pounded in Colin Buchanan's *Traffic in Towns*, 1964.

The Town and Country Planning Act 1968 provided for regularly revised local plans (responsibility for whose produc-tion fell to the new district councils established in 1974) and structure plans (the responsibility of regional councils). The large-canvas plan has its antecedent in the deliberations of the Clyde Valley Regional Planning Advisory Committee set up in 1927 and comprising the local planning authorities in Lanarkshire, Dumbartonshire and Renfrewshire. Their initial essays on roads and open spaces were followed by the encompassing *Clyde Valley Regional Plan* of 1946, a model for other regional plans which followed shortly after. Such plans are an acknowledgement of the interdependence of an urban area and its hinterland, which was taken a step further with the abolition of town councils in 1975. Today, with improved road networks, supermarket shopping and commuting, town life and country life have become almost indistinguishable. The concept of a region as an urban field has emerged, in which the core town is losing its traditional dominance.

Public congregation

The assembling together of human beings for communal activities has always had a special importance to mankind; so much so that it has been invested with spiritual significance, in the 'congregation' of the tribes of Israel for example. Our usage of the word, too, has a specific religious meaning. One of the fundamental features of town life is that it enables assembling to be easily accomplished, and consequently widens the range of circumstances and purposes for which congregation occurs. Congregation in the towns of the last two hundred years has taken novel forms. A burgh as originally conceived was what Lynch (1988) calls a 'single *corpus christianum*' with the town church as its spiritual centre. For hundreds of years this building with its surrounding churchyard served as notice board, town hall, court, playground and sports centre (for the popular golf, football and archery) – a symbolic cosmological focus of the community. The philosophy of individual enterprise gradually undermined this unity, creating, again in the words of Lynch (1988) a '*melange* of civic and occupational piety' centred upon the different interest groups of merchants and craftsmen. Masonic influences were particularly strong in Scotland and expanded during the nineteenth century. For the lodge offered a concept – *quasi*-religious, *quasi*-rationalistic – which struck a chord with men trying to come to terms with a new urban life style. An open masonic presence was common at official inaugurations of public buildings and works. Many buildings of the time were in fact erected through the enthusiasm and collective action of individuals, in contrast to the bureaucratic origin of later structures, and such group bonding was closely associated with the public growth of towns.

The simple lodge buildings of the eighteenth century were augmented by a more mysterious baronial and gothic in the Victorian period. The institution of freemasonry was echoed by similar organizations such as a number of national mutual security societies, including the Ancient Order of Foresters. They provided a primitive social security as well as the comfort of clubmanship and ritual. By contrast insurance companies such as the Prudential, with its distinctive exuberant baroque gothic buildings by Alfred Waterhouse, offered financial security without the opportunities of social congregation. Social security, health and unemployment benefits have put an end to friendly societies, though the masons still thrive. The clubbable have turned to the British Legion, Miners' Welfare or Labour Club for group solidarity.

Traditional pubs (and very numerous they were) had been little more than darkened rooms in enlarged houses. The first and second statistical accounts of the 1790s and 1830s are peppered with moral observations and statistical curiosity over their prevalence, Dunbar in East Lothian supposedly having the distinction of the greatest number per head of population (54 for 3,200 people in 1835). From the 1830s, however, gin palaces with plate glass windows, richly ornamented façades, gilded lettering and brilliant gas lights set the pattern for urban pubs which is still prevalent today (even if only as a fake reconstruction of decor which not so long ago was being stripped out for being old-fashioned). The brightness and enchantment would have been (as they were intended to be) in sharp contrast to the urban dwellings of their clientèle, just as the futuristic architecture of the cinema later promised worlds of fantasy as different as possible from the living and working conditions of the audience.

The new urban pubs were much larger and more functional than their forerunners, with long counters for ease and speed of service. Political and social congregation were supplemented by the attractions of entertainment – the music hall originated in large London pubs. The very powerful Victorian temperance movement (responsible for alternative coffee houses and experiments such as Gothenberg pubs) looked askance at (and probably found rather dangerous) the potent mixture of politics and drink, and a wedge was driven between the two by the invention of the off-licence, an institution whose success can be gauged by the numerous listings of 'spirit dealers' in High Street valuation rolls of the turn of the century. Politics were more safely tamed in the airiness of a new town hall, where dissent could be regulated by the rules of democratic debate. A look at newspaper reports of the time shows that the level of rowdiness at these meetings was quite excessive, not to mention the range of missiles swept up after the event. In Musselburgh Town Hall, for example, in March 1912, speakers were pelted with 'bundles of pease meal, soot, boiled potatoes, peas, rotten eggs and even cayenne pepper' such that the hall afterwards reminded one spectator of a 'bakehouse floor with the wall spattered all over with eggs and over ripe oranges' (quoted in Roberts and Wallace, 1989).

Those who worried about political revolution from the lower classes would have taken comfort from the late nineteenth-century enthusiasms for entertainment (music hall, then cinema) and sport, at the expense of self-improvement and mass-movement politics. The working class had hitherto lacked recreational facilities of the type favoured by the middle classes – such as the assembly rooms modelled on those of Bath and other fashionable spas built at the beginning of the nineteenth century in Edinburgh, Aberdeen, Dunbar and elsewhere. Some working men clubbed together to build recreation rooms, from which today's community centres are descended. A novelty introduced by the Victorian proletariat was the spectator sport – football especially – which led to the congregation of thousands through the turnstiles of stadia, in a regulated paradigm of organized industrial society. Even the rules of sport became as fixed as clocking in and clocking out, and no doubt the fears of the authorities, faced with the congregation of such numbers, were allayed by the comforting structure of ritualized competition.

Such structuring of a town's open spaces of assembly can also be seen in its parks, which replaced those open common lands that had been the scene of riots and political confrontation earlier in the nineteenth century. Daunton (1983) talks of 'the municipal park, with the careful delineation of recreation ground from flower beds, with keepers, bye-laws, specific hours of admission, booking procedure for pitches, and the pervasive iron railings'. The situation of such a park or recreation ground often coincides with a fixation line, that boundary on the edge of a town which marks the extent of development during a building cycle. Marginal land was available cheaply and could be purchased by town councils under powers in the Public Parks (Scotland) Act 1878. Frequently, land was also gifted by a local industrialist or landowner. Where the building cycle lagged behind burgh boundary extension, provision of parkland could be quite generous, as with Dundee's collection of Baxter Park, The Law, Dudhope Park, Balgay Park, Victoria Park and Lochee Park. Parkland is also associated with poor-quality central areas. The bog of Princes Street gardens is the most famous example; the nineteenth-century Alexandra Park for Glasgow's working class boasted 'air pollution so bad that only the hardiest species of trees and shrubs could survive' (Adams, 1978); whilst floodplains (as in Aberfeldy and Pitlochry) remain favourite recreation areas.

The public park for the use and enjoyment of all was a Victorian invention, and can be contrasted with the private locked gardens associated with Georgian terraces, as in Edinburgh's New Town. Examples such as Glasgow's Kelvingrove Park with its botanic antecedents and attendant cultural amenities scored highly on the list of desirabilia of Victorian suburbanites. 'Idealised landscapes at the edge of their fast growing towns', Chadwick (1966) calls them, 'standing aloof from the realities of life rather like the chaste, naked white marble statues which graced their withdrawing rooms. Such parks represented art and were morally instructive; they also represented science and gave practical instruction.'

The cultural and educational credentials of the likes of Kelvingrove may not have been very imaginatively translated to the run of the mill municipal park, but they did provide a source of inspiration to Patrick Geddes, the famous Scots pioneer of town planning and conservation. In his 1904 *City Development: A Study of Parks, Gardens and Culture-Institutes*, he argued that 'the last generation has had to carry out great work of prime necessity, as of water supply, sanitation and the like'; but that now the new concern was 'that of ensuring healthier conditions, of providing happier and nobler ones'. Geddes set out his ideas as landscape consultant to the Carnegie Dunfermline Trust for the laying out of Pittencrieff Park. His vision was at the opposite extreme from the iron railing mentality and sought for an integrated harmony between building and open space, applied to the townscape as a whole. 'Geddes' park', writes Chadwick, 'was the Victorian park . . . stuffed so full of various components that it was to be park, garden, zoological garden, botanic garden, recreation ground, open air museum, all rolled into one.'

The theme of congregation and the authorities' response to it can be pursued by the local historian up to the present day (even apparently harmless innovations such as coffee bars and ice cream parlours have been seen as a threat by some). It is certainly one of the more important aspects of urban living. Durkheim, the nineteenth-century pioneer of sociology, made an equation between moral density and physical density – the concentration of population to be found in towns made possible a range of contacts between individuals and groups, enhancing the potential for deeper intimacies and self-fulfilment. Others have considered towns more negatively: 'urban social life', says Daunton (1983), 'was increasingly carried on within specialist space controlled and regulated by its owner, whether commercial or municipal. The pattern of the late Victorian city was that people would assemble, but in a passive rather than participatory role, always under the control of a definite regulatory agency.'

Churches and cemeteries

Congregation has a specific connotation in ecclesiastical parlance – a reflection of the ancient importance of this form of assembly. The tradition was one which the nineteenth century strove intently to revive, and the anxiety for spiritual unity in a world increasingly fragmented by scientific rationality led to excessive architectural statement.

In the Scots vernacular tradition, sober medieval Gothic married to cottage simplicity, as found at Iona, had evolved through the square tower and cupola of the seventeenth century, to be reinterpreted afresh in the pleasing box structures of the Georgian period. There were even straight Gothic survivals such as Michael Kirk, Elgin (1705), now Gordonstoun School chapel. Even the flurry of enthusiasm for the Greek temple revival of the 1840s (an unlikely pagan model for Christian churches) was accommodated with some success, given the common denominator of the essential box shape and the compatibility of the austere Doric with the Calvinist mentality (the more ornate Greek styles usually work less well). A traditional location for town churches was either in the vicinity of the tolbooth (its sister authority in the organization of the burgh) or in a commanding or open position, often outside the town walls.

Contemporary with these Greek experiments, there began the great flowering of a gothic revival (English and continental rather than Scottish). Despite impeccable Christian credentials (indeed its greatest apologist A. W. Pugin saw its introduction as a crusade for the return of the ancient faith) it brought, with its transepts, spires and ornamentation, a totally exotic plant into the Scottish townscape, especially to its skyline. Incongruous too was its adoption of the trappings of English ecclesiastical style, with a nave and altar axis replacing the pulpit and gallery orientation.

Exoticism is one of the keys to the revival. Charles Eastlake, its Victorian historian, noted in his *History of the Gothic Revival* (1872) that 'it may seem strange that a style of design which is intimately associated with the romance of the world's history should now-a-days find favour in a country distinguished above all others for the plain business-like tenour of its daily life'. Of course, that was exactly the point – the soaring religious architecture was a compensation, though whether most of its buildings, soon to be covered with the industrial grime to which it was intended as an antidote, nowadays raise rather than depress the spirits is a question on which architectural historians seem to differ.

The extent of church building in the nineteenth century was quite prodigious; Glasgow's new West End, for example, boasted 29 by 1914 (one per thousand of population). The reasons were various. To Thomas Chalmers goes the credit of identifying the crisis in traditional parochial organization brought on by the explosive growth of towns at the start of the nineteenth century. Chalmers wrote *The Christian and Civil Economy of Large Towns* (1821–6), initiating a crusade in the new industrial suburbs. Extra urban parishes, known as *quoad sacra* parishes, were created in towns with populations of three or four thousand upwards to relieve pressure on the main parish church, and government funds were provided for new buildings. Thomas Telford, more famous as an engineer, built 32 between 1824 and 1840.

At the same time, an improving standard of living led many townspeople to look askance at their homely vernacular churches and to demand something more grand. A large number of parish churches were rebuilt in the first thirty years of the nineteenth century. A third factor was the bewildering history of secession and reunification within the Scottish churches, most notably the Disruption of 1843. A Free Church made its appearance in nearly every town in the space of a few years – a remarkable display of enthusiasm and fund raising. Other secession churches served congregations of the United Presbyterians formed by the amalgamation of the United Session and the Relief Church, and the United Free Church (after 1900) from the Free Church and United Presbyterians, leaving the invariable rumps to continue in yet more buildings. With subsequent reunifications, many of these churches will have been converted to other uses – church halls, warehouses, workshops and homes.

A fourth cause of church growth was the strong impact of external religious traditions, encouraged by the liberalization of belief and the new aspirations of an industrial working population. Catholic churches multiplied in areas of Irish immigration, and with English influences came strengthened episcopalianism, methodism and congregationalism; from the poorest in the community came evangelical millenarianism, also associated with groups set apart, such as fishermen with their mission halls.

Forced into a competitive jungle in the side streets, and lacking the sanction of an established status, all these numerous competing doctrines (facing too, as the century progressed, a growing public indifference to religion altogether) demanded buildings that drew attention to themselves, and encouraged an architectural rhetoric in place of the quiet confidence of a unified faith. Perhaps only the evangelical halls, sustained by the fervour of their penniless converts, remained modest or undemonstrative in their architecture. 'Religious sectarianism has its stylistic reflection' suggests F. A. Walker (1986) and points in illustration to a tight cluster of churches in Paisley's Oakshaw district. The group includes some neo-Gothic (St John's 1862–3 and the Congregational (1887) both in polychromatic style) joining the eighteenth-century High Church and Middle Church with their 'union of classicism and reformed religion', the pagan temple of Oakshaw East United Free Church (1826) and the 'lingering rigour of meeting house religion' in a much altered Old Gaelic Church (1793).

The first generation of Gothic revivalists favoured the perpendicular style, berated by Eastlake as debased, vulgarized and graceless in itself, and doubly so in its fanciful and inaccurate reinterpretation by revivalists. The style had the added appeal of cheapness, with walls as thin as structural safety would permit. Nevertheless the perpendicular, with its square towers, box structure and crenellated parapets, harmonized with Scottish tradition better than some of its successors. Examples are Kincardine Parish Church 1814–16, Clackmannan Parish Church (James Gillespie Graham, 1815) and Nigg Kirk, Aberdeen (John Smith 1828).

Detailed antiquarian studies reproduced in architectural manuals gave the following generation of architects more accurate models to reproduce: firstly Early English and fourteenth-century Gothic, and then versions of French and Italian. The latter provided an impetus for the revival towards original expression as it shook off, in Eastlake's words, 'the trammels of antiquarian precedent' or what Walker (1985) calls 'an era of wholesale cultural apostasy'. One of the most independent of the new architects was F. T. Pilkington, whose work has been seen as the epitome of the sublime. His English-and French-inspired 'savage' Gothic has been contrasted with the tepid picturesque of the perpendicular style. Examples of his work are McCheyne Memorial Church, Dundee, Barclay

Church, Edinburgh, St John's, Kelso and Trinity Church in Irvine. Also in the sublime mould are the Glasgow churches of Alexander 'Greek' Thomson, in Caledonia Road, St Vincent Street and Queen's Park.

One of the somewhat eccentric consequences of the revival was a taste for polychrome, with brick, marble and mosaic, whilst the turn of the century witnessed Art Nouveau reinterpretations, though still dominated by nave and transept. The resurgence of genuine Scottish gothic forms owed much to the careful drawings of R.W. Billings in his *The Baronial and Ecclesiastical Antiquities of Scotland*, Blackwood, 1845–52. Hippolyte Blanc's Coats' Memorial Church in Paisley has been considered an outstanding example. Romanesque (round arch) churches also established a rapport with the simplicity of native tradition, in examples at Dalmeny and Leuchars by Peter Macgregor Chalmers.

The dramatic impact of secularization on church architecture is also evident in the story of churchyards and cemeteries. One very practical problem was space, given the much greater concentrations of people: traditional churchyards soon became filled. A pioneering alternative was Glasgow's Necropolis of 1832, complete with Egyptian vaults. It was described by the Scottish landscape artist John Claudius Loudon in the *Gardener's Magazine* (1842) as being designed 'to invest with more soothing associations that affectionate recollection of the departed which is cherished by those who survive'. The secular overtones are even more explicit in his book *On the Laying Out, Planting and Management of Cemeteries* (1843), in which he saw the desirable relationship between the cemetery and its urban milieu as one contributing to 'the improvement of the moral sentiments and general taste of all classes, and more especially of the great masses of society'. The importance of urban space as a tool of social engineering has never been more clearly acknowledged than in this passage.

A mid-nineteenth-century parliamentary report considered the interment of the dead as a matter unfit for commercial speculation (many of the new cemeteries had been business ventures) and local authorities were made responsible for it, and for churchyards as well by the end of the century. A decline in the cemetery aesthetic has been attributed to public health concerns. Curl (1972) explains that formerly 'bodies had been crammed into small areas, and so graveyards did not impinge too much on the visual scene. When bodies were buried in single graves, however, and regulations controlled exhumation and the management of cemeteries, land was rapidly used and cemeteries became huge, utilitarian and ugly.'

Tombstones too have become standardized in their ugliness. The vigorous native carving tradition of the seventeenth and eighteenth centuries was supplanted by the machine-cut motifs of the nineteenth, displaying the same architectural eclecticism – Egyptian, Greek, Gothic – as the industrial towns in which they stood. Charles Knight referred in the 1840s to 'the stately Corinthian column, broken midway in its height' as a symbol of 'a noble type of man cast down in his prime' but pleaded for a return to the lost individuality of the mason's art. The designers of Victorian gravestones appear to have paid little heed, but their whimsical and theatrical exuberance at least produces what Curl (1972) calls a 'cluttered vitality totally lacking in today's regulation stones'. The prospect of joining their serried ranks (urban functionalism even in death) has led many to prefer cremation, legalized by an act of parliament in 1902.

Educational institutions

So long as the larger role of education was seen in terms of moral instruction and character formation rather than the imparting of knowledge or intellectual skills, public involvement remained equivocal. When schooling became a public responsibility in 1872, there was accordingly a considerable shortage of buildings. About three thousand children in Aberdeen, for example, attended no school at all. A building programme over the next twenty years led to the numerous 'Public Schools' or 'Board Schools' (named from the local authorities responsible – the school boards). Class photographs of the often shoeless children seem to survive in large numbers – most of the pupils would never have been photographed before. Checkland (1976) has pointed to 'the contrast between the large number of new, bright and airy schools provided by the Board and the dismal houses of so many of the pupils'.

The architecture of these schools favoured either a sort of gothic (on the strength of its associated Christian ethic), or a bare classical style, or the baronial. The native tradition was seen as an appropriate symbol of Scottish educational heritage; indeed the new schools followed, with scarcely a break, the vernacular tradition of the old burgh schools of the early nineteenth century (combining English, mathematical and grammar sections), whose modest scale was consistent with the low status of the schoolteacher. During the initial phase of the industrial revolution these had been joined by extra church/burgh schools known as side schools, parish schools and parliamentary schools, but they too were normally traditional, domestic-scale buildings.

More of an architectural flowering occurred in the development of the endowed foundation. Greek Doric, considered 'symbolic of high quality learning' (Swan, 1987) was favoured for Dollar Academy, Blythswood Testimonial School, Renfrew, Dundee's High School and Bell's Institution in Inverness as well as many others. Walker (1985) argues that mid-nineteenth-century college foundations were 'effectively a large house – often a country house . . . catering for the educational, physical and moral well-being of a greatly extended family'. Country house copies, following a gothic idiom overlaid with French château and Flemish influences, reached their apogee in Edinburgh's Fettes College, which has been described as 'possibly the most flamboyant French Gothic public building in the British Isles'. Other examples are Morgan Academy, Dundee and Crieff's Morrison's Academy. The financing of such magnificent edifices was made possible by the extensive urban land ownership of these foundations. These schools were a significant part of a very limited secondary education provision, for most pupils attended just the one Board school which they left at the age of 13, if not before. More widespread secondary education was dependent upon new local authority foundations, which were encouraged by state grants provided for in the 1908 Education Act.

The decline in the moral emphasis of education in favour of the acquisition of knowledge led to the incorporation of denominational schools into the state system – most importantly the Catholic schools in 1918. The architecture too has perhaps responded to the image of modernity fostered by secular learning.

The reluctance of the authorities to take responsibility for secondary education was, predictably, matched by an indifference to adult education. Self-help had been the watchword for mechanics' institutes formed by both employers and employees, mostly in the central belt. Their objective, in the words of one prospectus, was to educate working men 'in such branches of physical science . . . of practical advantage in their several trades'. A fine example of mechanics' institute premises is now the Bon Accord Hotel in Aberdeen. The libraries of the institutes looked askance on fiction, as did early public libraries. Not that there were many of the latter. The Public Library (Scotland) Act 1853 permitted burghs to canvass electors for the introduction of a penny rate. A majority vote settled the matter one way or another. Adoption by council resolution as opposed to referendum was not an option before 1894. Not much enthusiasm was shown until Andrew Carnegie, late in the century, offered the incentive of buildings or books provided voters accepted the penny rate. By 1914 half the population of Scotland was served by public libraries. The educative role of the library, reinforced by the powers given to education authorities in 1918 to provide a service, has only in recent years given way to a recreational emphasis. Museums have had a similar history, originating with learned society foundations in Perth, Paisley, Inverness, Elgin, Montrose and other places. The first municipally owned and administered museums were Victorian, early examples being Peterhead, Peebles, Airdrie, Kilmarnock and Wick. In contrast to libraries, however, private museums have continued to thrive alongside the many municipal foundations. Traditional library and museum buildings have tended to reflect their educational pretensions, with an abundance of classical allusion of one kind or another.

Social welfare

As the many engineering problems of the modern town, through the default of private enterprise, forced themselves upon the attention of local councils any slight chance that the social problems of industrial settlement would become an early or major focus of attention were scotched. A perfunctory poor relief, administered by non-elected parochial boards set up in 1845, left most of the work of social services to voluntary and charitable organizations.

Town councils, their churches and trade incorporations, had traditionally looked after their own in poverty and sickness. One still-standing monument to that age is the King

James VI hospital in Perth. Sites of early hospitals were often outside the back dykes (for instance Ayr's hospital in Mid Vennel) because of the lack of publicly owned land in the centre. Poor beggars from outside who flooded into the towns during times of famine were given short shrift; but the problem for the nineteenth-century town fathers was that their immigrants had come to stay.

Philanthropic hospital foundations were established on fringe belts, to be joined by public utilities and other functions demanding large amounts of space (such as cemeteries and golf courses). Centrally situated infirmaries provided a local service for the poor – the seriously ill were more likely to find themselves in hospital wards in poorhouses, built in large numbers from the mid-nineteenth century. Adams (1978) refers to them as 'penal-like institutions' whose 'isolation and cold grandeur must have brought terror to the heart of many a destitute person'.

The creation of larger public health authorities (district committees) under the county councils of 1889 led to hospital expenditure being quadrupled in five years. Many town councils were still reticent however. 'The negligence of the Kirkcaldy authorities to provide suitable hospital accommodation is I fear too typical of some at least among the small Scotch burghs' noted a Local Government Board official in 1896 (quoted in Levitt, 1988). Sometimes town and district authorities co-operated, as for example with the Renfrew and Clydebank Joint Hospital at Blawarthill. Much controversy at the time centred on the provision of 'fever' hospitals to accommodate epidemic victims. The logic of isolating sufferers from general hospital and poorhouse patients was slow to be accepted. Tents and huts were used in emergency, the latter often remaining as permanent isolation hospitals. The standard was still not high: 'one half of the ward block is used for the isolation of cases of Scarlet Fever' says a Report on the General Sanitary Condition of the Burgh of Hamilton in 1909, 'the other half is used for cases of Enteric Fever and Diphtheria' (quoted in Levitt, 1988). One child admitted with diphtheria contracted both enteric fever and scarlet fever.

The first general hospital provision in many of the smaller burghs was the small cottage hospital, often funded by benefaction around the turn of the century. Early examples in the west of Scotland are Dumbarton (1890), Johnstone (1893), Helensburgh (1895) and Rothesay (1891).

Transport and communications

In terms of the structure of towns a transport network serves both to connect and to direct. In the words of Forsyth (1982), 'cart traffic, horse omnibuses, and later the railways and tramways all sought to serve the area of greatest existing social and economic contact. In doing so they increasingly confirmed the superior accessibility of that area'. This is not to say that radical change does not occur. The military roads of the eighteenth century often cut across existing routes. New coach roads were equally ruthless, for example in Dalkeith (Edinburgh Road and South Street) and Dumfries (Church Street and Buccleuch Street). It was common at this time for old town gates to be demolished and central access roads to be widened. A strong radial structure is evident in most traditional towns, and it has been noted that only in exceptional cases of civic power and foresight were circumferential links made between radial routes through the growing inner suburban areas. The proliferation of the motor car has meant that axial development has been replaced by infill development as the importance of public transport has diminished. Glasgow's twentieth-century attempt at inner ring building ended in the disaster of the motorway going nowhere, but the planners can take comfort in the observation that 'transportation problems are virtually universal facets of urban growth' (Herbert and Thomas, 1982), or in Walker's (1986) judgment of Erskine as 'a disorientating network of roads' just like 'every other post war new town'. The strategy in both Glasgow's and Erskine's cases is to supply a network in order to *direct* economic development where before roads were simply built in *response* to economic pressures. The success or otherwise of such planning is central to assessing the effectiveness of public intervention.

The upkeep of roads by a public authority has never been questioned, possibly because good communications are essential if a state is to impose its will. Curiously, however, there was no early impetus to make railways a public responsibility, despite their impact on the landscape and economy. A careful scrutiny of the route taken by a railway into a town centre will reveal much to the local historian about the character of that town. For the railway, in the words of an American visitor in the 1860s, enters 'as you would a farmer's house if you first passed through the pig-stye into the kitchen' (quoted in Simmons, 1973). More often than not 'the pig-styes' concerned were working-class residential districts, which were sacrificed to the railway much as they have been more recently to the urban motorway. Such areas constituted a 'line of least resistance', preferable even to commercial and industrial sectors. Those evicted had little chance of moving into different areas, for they were dependent on obtaining casual labour. The resulting overcrowding was exacerbated by the goods yards and factories that gravitated to the rail side. In the Gorgie area of Edinburgh, Naismith (1989) estimates that railways and sidings carved up an area equal in size to the whole of the New Town. One effect was to drive up land values, directly through the railway's own land hunger, and indirectly through improved accessibility.

The very centre of a town was more often than not unconquered by the railway, partly because of the unwilling-ness of landowners to sell. The unwillingness was both aesthetic (as witnessed by the battle for Princes Street gardens, finally won by the railway at the cost of constructing a tunnel and deep cutting) and economic, for central sites would normally be already yielding high rents. One consequence was that few towns of any size achieved Aberdeen's feat of concentrating its incoming railways into one station.

The arrival of a railway system in a burgh is mixed in its effects. Certainly those towns which it bypassed suffered relative decline. But so, equally, did some of those it did reach, for the more remote areas in particular found their old-fashioned craft economies subject to the competition of cheap factory-made goods. Of course, where local conditions were favourable the process could work in reverse, to the advantage of the younger industrial town.

Architecturally, the wrought iron of railway stations was one of the original contributions of the Victorian age, the two Glasgow stations of St Enoch's and Queen Street being good examples. The ironwork was often married to a baronial style, as in Dundee's Caledonian Station; while Stirling has been described as one of the loveliest of Scottish stations, with crowstep gables and 'crenellated freak-Edwardian charm' (McKean, 1985).

Public utilities

Asa Briggs has suggested that 'the hidden network of pipes

and drains and sewers in Victorian towns was one of the biggest technological and social achievements of the age' (quoted in McKichan, 1978). Its obverse was a neglect of architectural beauty above ground; even, in Mumford's (1966) view, an extension 'of the principle of the underground city . . . to the design of buildings'. Yet the cost of public works, and the burden on the rates, provided ammunition for a century-long rearguard action of opposition, such that in Kirkcaldy, as late as 1903, the medical officer of health reported that the town's water supply presented 'a grave danger to public health'; yet still the council prevaricated.

Dundee's so-called water war lasted from 1832 to 1874, when the principal supply from Lintrathen was established after years in which smallpox, typhus, typhoid and gastric fevers had claimed 300–500 lives per annum. The statistic is not surprising when one learns that a water commission of 1868 found the pleasant piquancy of Dundee's water due to 'a very purified sewage'. As elsewhere the merchants and tradesmen opposed a water rate on the grounds that 'they did not see the peculiar circumstances that should make men idiots enough to prefer paying by taxation what ought to be vendible in the market like any other commodity'. Such an argument is of course back in the centre of debate in our own day.

Stirling's inhabitants reasoned, as reported by a waterworks committee in 1844, that the policy of little local taxation 'had been a great means of bringing respectable inhabitants to the town and they ought to take care how they encroached upon that privilege' (quoted by McKichan, 1978). However, such views became increasingly irrelevant with the growing understanding of water-borne diseases, particularly those that hit at rich and poor indiscriminately. There is a marked variation in the response of different burghs – some for example had obtained local acts of parliament to levy rates via police commissioners (Canongate as early as 1772, Greenock 1773, Glasgow 1800, Edinburgh 1805, Paisley 1806, Gorbals 1808, Kilmarnock 1810 and Perth and Dunfermline 1811). The general police acts mentioned elsewhere in this book gave permissive powers, but no compulsion, as did the Waterworks Clauses acts of 1847 and 1863.

Traditional urban water supply came from manual draw wells or was brought from a river, as at Dumfries. Wooden pipes of elm (cheap, but lasting only about 30 years) brought water from more distant springs, until the introduction of the cast iron pipe in the mid-eighteenth century. This was a time of other innovations – the Newcomen steam engine and its successors the Cornish pumping engines improved reservoir and filtering systems, and traditional cisterns were enlarged to reservoirs. At the street level, old conduits and wells were replaced or augmented by pumps, which can be seen in many Victorian photographs.

The modern systems which were developed in Victorian times improved on the traditional settling method of purification (which takes place naturally as the water lies in the reservoir) by filtration, firstly through sand beds but more recently with pressure filtration through steel drums containing sand under pressure.

Location of storage tanks and reservoirs is crucial, as the difference between their height above sea level and that of the users' premises dictates the available pressure. Perching them on hillsides above towns has been the obvious engineering solution. Perth's early scheme (1829–32) showed more originality. The water was pumped by steam from the river Tay into a high water tank in a still-standing classical rotunda, whence it was piped to residences in the lower part of the town.

Rising levels and sophistication of demand increasingly made local sources of supply inadequate and led to schemes for bringing water from mountain reservoirs. Because of their more ambitious scale, commissioners from more than one authority often shared projects as combination water trusts. This trend continued in the inter-war years with the formation of county-wide water boards, reduced to 13 for the whole of Scotland by the Water (Scotland) Act of 1967.

Water supply was the most crucial of public utilities, not only because it was in itself essential for healthy living, but also because, as the nineteenth-century sanitary reformers never tired of pointing out, a good supply of piped water was a prerequisite for the equally vital sewage system. It also made possible public baths and wash houses.

It has been suggested that the reluctance to accept sanitary improvement was not merely political. 'Never before', suggests Schoenwald (1973), 'had a systematic attempt been made to interfere with an intimate human function'. It is certainly true that Edwin Chadwick, the leading protagonist, pursued an obsessive quest to recapture the physical care shown by a dead mother, and foresaw a network of pipes so fully branched that no man could declare himself free of its tentacles. 'Sewers below and water closet above . . . all performing with discipline, not once a year or once a month but several times each day.'

The separation of domestic refuse from excreta was the minimum improvement sought by Victorian inspectors. In Kilmarnock in 1856 it was reported that 'heaps of rotting filth are accumulated in back courts, exposed to the fermenting action of sun and rain while around them little children play unconcernedly, rolling about on the poisoned soil and inhaling the disease-laden air'; and a recommendation was put to the town council to draw up plans for ashpits with detached privies. Such a system, it was reported, was operational in Edinburgh and Montrose with a daily night-time collection removed by rail, the contents of the privy pails being emptied into the middle of the truck on top of the ashes and refuse. This is a description of the so-called 'dry closet' system, operating with an army of 'night soil men'.

Flushing WCs were introduced late in the nineteenth century, though widespread adoption of them in working-class housing was tardy. A report on Port Glasgow's Improvement Scheme in 1903 noted in one area a provision of only 13 WCs and two 'objectionable privies' serving a population upwards of 2,000. The 1892 to 1903 Burgh Police acts gave powers to compel house owners to connect a town's water supply and sewers.

Nationalization, North Sea gas and the national grid have obscured the homely origins of gas and electricity generation. Old photographs show councillors posing proudly in front of their small burgh gasometers (often built at or near the sea to provide maximum atmospheric pressure on the holder). Gas was introduced to Edinburgh in 1812 and quickly spread, its advent predating the municipalization controversies. Initial providers were joint stock companies operating local monopolies. House lighting was limited by the lack of an effective mantle before 1885 (gas's equivalent of the light bulb), so the underbelly of nineteenth-century towns was not criss-crossed with gas pipes: these were concentrated in prestige locations, for street lighting and shop display. Municipal control was authorized by the Burgh Gas Supply (Scotland) Act 1876. Free cookers and cheap hire of gas fires brought the number of consumers in the four big cities to well over a quarter of a million by the end of the century.

Electricity proved more significant, for three reasons. Though more costly than steam power, it could be transmitted with greater ease and in more variable amounts – it thus had industrial potential. Secondly, it proved ideal for powering tramways – the first rapid street transport system. Thirdly, suburbanites benefited from electric light and an increasing range of electrical appliances. 'How often our customers say, "Why didn't I have power plugs installed when I was wiring my house for lighting?" ' is the rhetorical question asked by the *Lothians Electric Power Company Bulletin* of the mid-1920s. The same bulletin was promoting the hire of electric cookers, irons, fires, kettles, toasters, vacuum cleaners and radios. The Lothians Electric Power Company (with 155 sub-stations) was one of several which operated on a large scale under local authority regulations.

The logic of a council 'taking over those public utilities that needed to dig up the streets' (Fraser, 1985) led Glasgow in 1899 to obtain a licence to set up its own telephone service. Within a year there were 4,000 subscribers. Telephone wires of course have been a notable urban feature above the ground. The growth of all these utilities has taken them far away from local control, though their impact on the modern town has been profound.

Local government records

Royal burghs apart, most Scottish towns will have few records before the nineteenth century. Burghs of barony, lacking an automatic right to a town council, often had no proceedings to minute; and police burghs date only from the second quarter of the century. The minute books of their commissioners are converted to town council minute books after the reforms of 1900. It must also be borne in mind that police commissioner records will also appear in royal burgh archives where local police acts had been adopted under the 1833 Burgh Police Act or where the council had promoted a local act of parliament. The cities in particular preferred to adopt powers through local act, taking a pride in pre-empting national developments. It was Scotland's small burghs whose standards were woefully lacking in, for example, sanitation.

The widening of local authority responsibility is reflected in a growth of committee and sub-committee minutes. A typical burgh might have a town hall or public buildings committee, harbour commissioners, a burial ground committee, a gas committee perhaps expanded later to include electricity, an epidemic hospital committee, a cottage hospital management committee and even committees for public parks, science and arts, public baths, footways and watching, lighting and fire engines. Housing committees became a necessity after the start of council house building programmes after World War One.

It has already been noted that town councils were by no means the sole authorities with responsibilities in urban areas. The records of most of the *ad hoc* bodies are now subsumed in county council archives. County councils established in 1889 also inherited many of the functions (and the records) of their predecessors, the commissioners of supply, a committee of major local landowners responsible, among other things, for highways. County council archives include most of the school records after 1872 (minute books of school boards and the vivid and popular school log books) and of the larger *ad hoc* education authorities of 1918–29.

Poor relief and poorhouses were the concern of parochial boards, founded in 1845 on a parish basis, though the boards worked in conjunction with town councils. A remit for public health and hospital provision accrued to the boards, which were replaced by fully elected parish councils in 1894. Electioneering for all these bodies was a novelty vigorously entered into by the middle classes, and the propaganda literature often survives to supplement the newspaper debates. In 1929 parish councils were abolished and replaced by district councils, based on larger areas encompassing both urban and landward areas. The group of records emanating from these different bodies includes the minute books of poorhouse committees (subsequently social welfare committees), public assistance committees, water boards and public library committees, as well as joint committees of town and district councils. The latter are one of the consequences of the overlap of functions.

The same is true of county councils themselves, where the position is further complicated by their different status vis-à-vis different categories of burgh after 1929. As already mentioned, the all-purpose town councils of the 1892–1903 acts were replaced by three groups – the four major cities which were granted county council status, so-called large burghs with a population of more than 20,000 and numerous small burghs which retained limited responsibilities. County and district councils supplied their other services through a range of sub-committees as extensive as those of town councils – those of road trustees, prison boards, hospitals, public buildings, police, weights and measures, water supply, drainage, building development, and piers and bridges. Both town and county council archives also have useful runs of annual reports by key officials such as sanitary inspectors, medical officers of health and chief constables.

The period since the Second World War, whilst it left the status of the three categories of burgh unchanged until 1974, has seen the erosion of many local government powers. The nationalization that took public utilities out of the local sphere has already been mentioned. Similarly, the introduction of the National Health Service transferred hospital provision to regional health boards. Poor relief became in large measure the responsibility of the government's Department of Health and Social Security.

Supervision of local authorities had begun with the establishment of the Scottish Board of Supervision in 1845 to monitor the work of parochial boards. In 1894 it was renamed the Local Government Board, by which time the Scottish Office had been established. Its supervision of all aspects of local authority work makes it an important source of records for the local historian of towns over the last hundred years. The names and precise functions of its different departments have changed over the years but their records can roughly be divided into three main groups – the education records of the originally named Scotch Education Department, town planning and economic development records under the umbrella of what is now the Scottish Development Department, and social welfare records, including housing and public health, under what was once the Home and Health Department. Most of these records are released for public use under the 'thirty year' rule, and can be consulted in the West Register House of the Scottish Record Office in Charlotte Square, Edinburgh. Records of nationalized industries in Scotland, together with their forerunners (thus including railway, gas and electricity companies) are also held in West Register House.

All these records provide plenty of opportunities for research. A comparison of buildings of similar function, from burgh to burgh and period to period, can illustrate the architectural and social outlook of the builders. The reuse of buildings, from poorhouses to churches, can be a study of imaginative adaptation. The proportion of public building and public space in a town can be analysed; also how the space was used, and by whom (all of the population or certain groups only). Rules and regulations including bye-laws seem to have great survival value – they can be studied to show aspects of authority and control. The diverse consequences of a new utility – the telephone, say – can be pursued, in the way business was done, letters written, premises located. Public congregation in different circumstances can be compared – what, for example, did football spectators have in common with the church assembly or the political meeting? Social history can take in the study of community facilities – the story of a club or town hall and the groups who used it (there are often plenty of old fancy dress and amateur dramatic photos available). In politics a lot of insight can be gained from interviewing members of old town councils and their provosts (their number now dwindling); and letters to the press are excellent for finding out about political attitudes – one would expect a feeling of group solidarity to be common to all three sources. One can look too at the attitude of the authorities to congregation – which kinds did they favour and promote (with grants and premises, for example) and which did they block? The reasons why are also very interesting to study. One could go on – indeed, the study of towns is as rich as the humanity contained in them and all its works. It was suggested elsewhere in this book that the town satisfies many human aspirations and instincts, though of course it may inhibit and distort others. Either way, the subject matter is ourselves, and a continuing object of our curiosity.

NOTES AND FURTHER READING

Chapter One, pp. 9–32

Bibliography of urban studies

Much of the impetus for urban studies in Britain has come from the work of Jim Dyos and the Urban History Group. Their *Urban History Newsletter* paved the way for the *Urban History Yearbooks* published annually since 1974 by Leicester University Press. Each volume includes reviews of periodical articles, recent theses and books, plus a current bibliography of around 1,000 indexed items. A bibliographical survey also appears as Chapter One of DYOS (1968), one of two major anthologies of the mid-1960s, the other being HAUSER, PHILIP & SCHNORE, LEV, *The Study of Urbanization: historiography through oral history*, Wiley, 1965. Subsequent overviews include STAVE, B. M., *The Making of Urban History*, SAGE, 1977; and FRASER & SUTCLIFFE (1983) of which the chapter by HERSHBERG, THEODORE, 'The future of urban history', pp. 428–48, includes in its notes a detailed bibliography of urban social literature. The chapter by STAVE, BRUCE M., 'A view from the United States', pp. 402–27, outlines the development of the subject and key works in that country.

There are two journals devoted to the subject – *Urbanism Past and Present* and *Journal of Urban History*, of which the June issue contains an annual bibliography of publications. Many other periodicals will also frequently contain relevant contributions, such as *Victorian Studies* and *Journal of Historical Geography*. There are several recent monographs on urban geography and urban historical geography, a few of which are listed in the references to this book.

PORTER, S., *Sources of Urban History*, Batsford, 1990 (published as this book was going to press) outlines the (mainly English) source materials available.

An early bibliography of studies of British towns was GROSS, CHARLES, *A Bibliography of British Municipal History*, New York, 1897 to which there is a supplementary volume by MARTIN, G. H., & MCINTYRE, SYLVIA, covering 1897–1966.

A bibliography of the social history of British cities is by GLASS, RUTH, 'Urban sociology in Great Britain: a trend report', *Current Sociology*, IV, No. 4, 1955, pp. 5–76. A survey of British research is by DENNIS, RICHARD & PRINCE, HUGH, 'Research in British urban historical geography', in DENEKE & SHAW (1988) pp. 9–23.

Scottish bibliography

A comprehensive bibliography of both book and non-book Scottish literature is the annual *Bibliography of Scotland* published by the National Library of Scotland since 1976–7. Publication from the late 1980s is on microfiche and cumulated annually. The standard bibliographies for earlier years are:

MITCHELL, ARTHUR & CASH, CALEB GEORGE, *A Contribution to the Bibliography of Scottish Topography*, 2 volumes, Constable, 1917.

HANCOCK, PHILIP DAVID, *A Bibliography of Works Relating to Scotland 1916–50*, 2 volumes, Edinburgh University Press, 1959–60.

Published volumes of old burgh records, including those of the nineteenth-century Scottish Burgh Records Society, are listed in:

STEVENSON, DAVID & WENDY, *Scottish Texts and Calendars: an analytical guide to serial publications*, Royal Historical Society/ Scottish History Society, 1987.

Scottish journals such as *Scottish History Review* and *Scottish Economic and Social History* include annual bibliographies and reviews. A general introductory source guide is:

MOODY, DAVID, *Scottish Local History: an introductory guide*, Batsford, 1986. Probably the most detailed bibliographical source for any particular locality is the catalogue of the local studies department of the library authority (in most cases the District Council). Few of these catalogues have been published.

Pictorial sources

There are some major photographic archives in Scotland. St Andrews University collections include those of Valentine & Sons Ltd (157,000), George Cowie (99,000), Robert M. Adam (14,000), six further individual collections and miscellaneous additions (a further 10,000). The glass negatives of George

Washington Wilson (40,000) are housed in Aberdeen University Library. Some notable collections are held in public libraries, for example that of Alexander Wilson who photographed Dundee and surrounding area between 1870 and 1900. Dundee Public Library also holds a complete photographic survey of industry, education and buildings carried out in 1916. Other library authorities boast substantial miscellaneous collections of photographs and postcards – Falkirk for instance with over 16,000. Details of these collections, plus all the other materials held in local history libraries are given in: *Exploring Scottish History: A Directory of Resource Centres for Scottish Local and National History in Scotland,* Scottish Local History Forum, 1992.

A large number of published volumes of local photographs has appeared in the last few years, some from library and museum authorities and others from commercial publishers. The most extensive series is published by the Dutch-based European Library, who have reproduced postcard collections for innumerable burghs, illustrated with text by local enthusiasts. A series of George Washington Wilson photographs, arranged thematically, has been published by Dalesman Books. Batsford have published many Scottish volumes in their *'Edwardian and Victorian . . . in old photographs'* series.

BYATT (1978) includes a detailed bibliography of books on postcards as well as a comprehensive directory of postcard publishers.

There have been interesting pieces written about some of the finds of old negatives, including two by George Oliver about what is now known as the Jackson collection in Glasgow University Archives:

OLIVER, GEORGE, 'Who held the camera? the Lind Collection', *Scots Magazine,* January 1980, pp. 406–17.

OLIVER, GEORGE, 'High days and holidays: the Lind collection II', *Scots Magazine,* February 1980, pp. 500–6.

The same author has written an absorbing introductory guide to pictorial sources for local historians, using many of the Jackson photographs in illustration:

OLIVER, GEORGE, *Photographs and Local History,* Batsford, 1989.

Other finds and collections are described in:

BURGESS, DAVID, 'The pictures from the potting shed', *Scots Magazine* January 1985 pp. 378–86

FISHER, J. A., *A Guide to the Published Photography of Thomas Annan,* Mitchell Library, 1977.

An index of photographers is the subject matter of:
STEVENSON, SARA & MORRISON-LOW, ALISON, *Scottish Photography*, Salvia Books, 1990.

Aerial shots are a category of photographs with distinctive values, combining the advantages of maps with visual representation. An unusual pioneer drawing of Aberdeen by George Washington Wilson in the 1850s from an aerial perspective is an early appreciation of the value of this combination. Aerofilms Ltd, Gate Studios, Station Road, Borehamwood, London were commercial pioneers of the picture postcard with oblique and vertical air camera. Aerial surveys organized through Cambridge University introduced systematic photography for archaeological purposes, and latterly similar surveys have covered the whole of Scotland as part of the work of the Royal Commission on the Ancient and Historical Monuments of Scotland. The records are held with the Archaeological Section of the National Monuments Record in Coates Place, Edinburgh.

Another visual record whose importance is being increasingly appreciated is film, and much is being preserved by the Scottish Film Council, Dowanhill, 74 Victoria Crescent Road, Glasgow G12 9JN. The Council's policy of copying on to video, much of which is subsequently available for purchase or loan, is contributing greatly to the accessibility of archive footage, and it is to be congratulated on its work and the helpfulness of its staff.

Sources for Scottish studies

Introductory surveys of Scottish urban history are not numerous, the pre-industrial town attracting the larger share of attention. The indispensable companion for all local researchers should be ADAMS (1978), which is based on a mountain of research in nineteenth- and twentieth-century town records. MCWILLIAM (1975) and NAISMITH (1989) share the perspective of the architectural historian.

A compendium of sociological studies is:
MCCRONE, D., KENDRICK, S. & STRAW, P., *The Making of Scotland: nation, culture and social change*, Edinburgh University Press, 1989.

Detailed work on the pre-industrial town is included in LYNCH (1988), whilst the seventeenth century is the focus of the very readable and stimulating MAIR (1988). Sources not cited in the text are:

EWAN, ELIZABETH, *Town Life in Fourteenth Century Scotland*, Edinburgh University Press, 1990.

GORDON, GEORGE & DICKS, BRIAN, *Scottish Urban History*, Aberdeen University Press, 1983.

LYNCH, MICHAEL, *The Early Modern Town in Scotland*, Croom Helm, 1987.

BROOKS, N. P., 'Urban Archaeology in Scotland', in BARLEY, M. W., *European Towns: their archaeology and early history*, Council for British Archaeology/Academic Press, 1977 notes that 'archaeology is a vital source of information for the history of Scottish towns, particularly during the Middle Ages when we have few documentary sources, no town maps and almost no surviving town houses'. The major archaeological response began with the publication in 1972 of the Urban Archaeology Committee of the Society of Antiquaries of Scotland's *Scotland's Medieval Burghs*. Subsequently, the Department of Archaeology at Glasgow University was sponsored to produce a series of reports on historic towns, known as the Scottish Burgh Survey, with the aim of identifying 'those areas within the burghs which were developed at various periods of their history up to approximately 1800 . . .' Reports on all Scotland's historic towns have followed, and should be available from local library authorities. In the forefront today is the work of the Scottish Urban Archaeology Trust Ltd, 55 South Methven Street, Perth, the successor to the Urban Archaeology Unit created in 1978 under the auspices of the Society of Antiquaries of Scotland. Archaeological reports are to be found in the annual volumes of the *Proceedings* of the Society, in journals of local antiquarian societies and in *ad hoc* reports of different excavations. Interim reports on most excavations are available through the Scottish Urban Archaeology Trust.

Sources for the nineteenth- and twentieth-century town

Research aids for the various categories of materials discussed in the text are as follows:

census data   BARKE, MICHAEL, 'Census enumeration books and the local historian', *Local Historian*, Volume 10 No. 5, February 1973 (a microlevel analysis of one street in Falkirk).

local acts	*Index to Local and Personal Acts 1801–1947*, HMSO, 1949 (with supplementary index for the years 1948–66, published in 1967).
newspapers	FERGUSON, JOAN P. S., *Directory of Scottish Newspapers*, National Library of Scotland, 1984 (gives locations of all known holdings of Scottish newspapers).
	NORTH, JOHN S., *The Waterloo Directory of Scottish Newspapers and Periodicals 1800–1900*, North Waterloo Academic Press, 2 volumes, 1989 (indexes a range of journals covering science, education, sport, home, church etc; also lists directories and almanacs)
commissions	FORD, P. & G., *Hansard's Catalogue and Breviate of Parliamentary Papers 1698–1834*, Irish University Press, 1968.
	FORD, P. & G., *Select List of Parliamentary Papers, 1837–99*, Blackwell, 1953.
	FORD, P. & G., *A Breviate of Parliamentary Papers 1900–1916*, Blackwell, 1957.
	FORD, P. & G., *A Breviate of Parliamentary Papers 1917–1939*, Blackwell, 1951.
	FORD, P. & G., *A Breviate of Parliamentary Papers 1940–1954*, Blackwell, 1961.
	FORD, P. & G., *Select List of Parliamentary Papers 1955–1964*, Irish University Press, 1970.
	MARSHALLSAY, DIANA & SMITH, J. H., *Ford List of British Parliamentary Papers 1965–1974*, KTO Press, 1979.
	This invaluable series provides a complete bibliographical coverage of parliamentary select committees and commissions. A simple guide to the maze of these records is:
	FORD, P. & G., *A Guide to Parliamentary Papers*, Irish University Press, 1972.
maps	a detailed catalogue of pre-Ordnance Survey mapping in Scotland is contained in:
	MOIR, D. G., *The Early Maps of Scotland to 1850*, Royal Scottish Geographical Society, Volume 1, 1973, Volume 2, 1983.
	The guide contains a note of all town maps; volume two is devoted to the innumerable plans of facilities (harbours, railways, etc.).

Some of the holdings of the Scottish Record Office (all their maps and plans are held together in West Register House) are listed in four volumes of inventories:

Descriptive List of Plans in the Scottish Record Office, HMSO, Volume 1, 1966, Volume 2, 1970, Volume 3, 1974, Volume 4, 1988.

A complete set of Ordnance Survey maps at all scales is held by the National Library of Scotland in its Map Room in the Causewayside building, 33 Salisbury Place, Edinburgh.

A third important national repository of maps and plans is the National Monuments Record, Coates Place, Edinburgh.

Local history libraries, archive offices, and the planning departments of local authorities will normally have extensive local collections. A recent guide to the use of maps is:

HINDLE, PAUL, *Maps for Local History*, Batsford, 1988.

Types of town

A form of town similar to the burgh of barony was the burgh of regality – the difference lay in the wider authority of the superior (for example the right to inflict the death penalty).

One small category of burgh created in 1833 was the parliamentary burgh (Paisley, Greenock, Leith, Kilmarnock, Falkirk, Hamilton, Peterhead, Musselburgh, Airdrie, Port Glasgow, Cromarty, Portobello and Oban). These were towns which were not traditional royal burghs and yet were of some size, so they were given parliamentary status to allow them to elect MPs to the reformed parliament of 1832. In the Burgh Police (Scotland) Act 1847 these burghs were also given the right, previously restricted to royal burghs and burghs of barony (Burgh Police (Scotland) Act 1833), to establish commissioners for the policing etc of their towns.

The status of all burghs established up to 1846 (no less than 482 in total) are listed in:

PRYDE, G. S., *The Burghs of Scotland: a critical list*, Oxford University Press, 1965.

A note on population of burghs

Researchers who, quite understandably, set out to establish the population growth of their towns as a prelude to the study of their development can encounter unexpected problems because of the overlapping categories of burgh status outlined above. For example, a royal burgh might have different boundaries from the parliamentary constituency established for it in 1832. The 1833 Police Act allowed the magistrates to establish a third status, of police burgh, with in 1847 the right to absorb these police powers into itself, as a municipal burgh. The consequence is that a town in the 1840s can have up to four different population figures, for royal, parliamentary, police and municipal burghs. Distinctions continued into the twentieth century.

This problem is compounded by regular extension of burgh boundaries as towns grew. Where the expansion was into green areas, population growth continued on a smooth path. Where, however, complete independent burghs were absorbed (as with Leith into Edinburgh), the apparent explosive growth in population is misleading for the historian.

Urban biography

Urban biographies or studies of specific towns appear in reasonable numbers from the first part of the nineteenth century. The early focus is very much on kings, earls and battles – the impinging of national affairs on the locality. Victorian historians, by contrast, delighted in the idiosyncracy of their towns and inhabitants, as well as expressing their new-found democratic rights in an enthusiasm for water supply, gas works, housing and amenity. Their works are full of detail, though not much historical analysis. The current generation has been the first to equal the Victorians in its passion for local history, and today's productions are much influenced by historical geography, as well as having a rigorous regard for scientific disciplines. As Asa Briggs suggests (1968) a perfect urban biography is a tall order. A lot of the best Scottish work is published by John Donald, with recent biographies of Irvine, Linlithgow, St Andrews, Stirling, Leith, Ayr, Aberdeen and Anstruther. Parthenon Publishing produced a fine study of Clydebank, a compilation entitled *The History of Clydebank*, 1988. Aberdeen University

Press publish volumes under the aegis of the Aberdeen University Centre for Scottish Studies.

Getting started in local research

Joining a local history society provides a good introduction. Your local library should have names and addresses of contacts; many societies are also attached to the umbrella organization, Scottish Local History Forum. The forum publishes a magazine, *Scottish Local History*.

The next step is to visit the local history library run by your local authority, plus the museums, record and archive offices in your area (see page 156–7). Your library can provide reading lists: the source that is often suggested at the outset is the three *Statistical Accounts* of Scotland that punctuate its history over the last two hundred years (1790s, 1830s/1840s and 1950s onwards). An account is written for each parish. GROOME, FRANCIS H., *Ordnance Gazetteer of Scotland*, 6 volumes, Thomas Mackenzie, 1882–5 is an exceptional gazetteer with succinct histories of each town's development.

There are other societies which all who care passionately for their towns might consider joining. Civic trust and civic heritage societies are often affiliated to the Scottish Civic Trust, 24 George Square, Glasgow. Both the Saltire Society, 9 Fountain Close, High Street, Edinburgh and the Architectural Heritage Society of Scotland, 43b Manor Place, Edinburgh take a strong interest in buildings old and new.

The main national centre for Scottish archives is the Scottish Record Office in Princes Street, Edinburgh (opposite the General Post Office in an elegant Adam building). A second building, West Register House, is situated in Charlotte Square and is the home for the plan collection and Scottish Office records. The Record Office publishes various leaflets outlining different areas of its holdings.

There are several directories that give information about the records and archives held by different institutions:

Exploring Scottish History: A Directory of Resource Centres for Scottish Local and National History in Scotland. Scottish Local History Forum, 1992.

FOSTER, J. & SHEPPARD, J., *British Archives: a guide to archive resources in the United Kingdom*, Macmillan, 1989.

Record Repositories in Great Britain, 8th edition, Royal Commission on Historical Manuscripts (HMSO), 1987.

Scottish Library and Information Resources, Scottish Library Association, *National Monuments Record of Scotland Jubilee: A Guide to the Collections 1941–1991*, HMSO, 1991.

Museums often have fine archive collections, particularly of photographs. They are listed in:
Scottish Museums and Galleries: the guide, Scottish Museums Council/Aberdeen University Press, 1990.

One topic not pursued in the text is the interpretations of Scottish townscape, homes and inhabitants by artists, for example by the school known as the Glasgow Boys. Many such works hang in local museums and art galleries.

Chapter Two, pp. 33–49

An Introduction to Scottish Legal History, Stair Society, 1958 is a fine introduction to aspects of the law of property ownership. Texts of all the relevant parliamentary legislation from earliest times to the end of the nineteenth century are contained in:
CRAIGIE, JOHN, *Conveyancing Statutes from the Thirteenth Century to the Present Time*, W. Green, 1895.

The development of the sasine registers is charted in:
RODGER, RICHARD & NEWMAN, JENNIFER, 'Property transfer and the Register of Sasines: urban development in Scotland since 1617', In *Urban History Yearbook* 1988, Leicester University Press, 1988, pp. 49–57.
Scottish Record Office leaflet No. 19 is *Indexes in the Historical Search Room to Deeds, Sasines and Testamentary Records.*

Sasine terminology

As well as the terms discussed in the text, the following transactions may be frequently encountered. They are shown with the commonly used abbreviations in the abridged registers.

Adj(udication) in imp(lement)	records an enforced sale or disposition in security when a seller reneges on a contract
Assig(nation)	transfer of a right (often a bond) to a new bondholder
Assumption, Deed of	the adoption of new trustee(s) or business partner(s)
Bond of Annuity	obliges payment of an annual sum to the grantee (very common with widows)

Bond of Cash Credit	Bond in favour of a bank for repayment of advances to a customer (linked with a disposition in security)
Bond of Corrob(oration) & Disp(osition)	a consolidation or renegotiation of existing bonds
Bond & Disp(osition) in Security	a 'mortgage' – replaced since 1970 by the 'standard security'
Bond of Provision	A bond providing for the future interests of others (often children and dependants)
Ch(arter) Resig(nation) G.S.	inheritance by general service
Cognition	inheritance
Decree	a decree is a court judgment (a judgment affecting property interests would be recorded in sasine)
Disch(arge)	cancellation of a burden, especially a bond in disposition and security
Disp(osition) & Assig(nation)	a straightforward disposition affected by a technicality of infeftment
Disp(osition) & Settl(ement)	inheritance bequeathed in testament
Excambion, Contract of	an agreement to exchange
Extract of. . . .	a copy of a legal document (e.g. a court decree) sanctioning an action by the grantee (in our case recording of title)
Extract Dec(ree) of Sp(ecial) Ser(vice)	inheritance
Extract Dec(ree) by Sheriff of Chancery	inheritance (usually lands held direct from the Crown)
Extract Gen(eral) Trust Disp(osition) & Settl(ement)	transfer of property to trustees by testament
Extract Dec(ree) of Gen(eral) Serv(ice)	inheritance

Extract Dec(ree) of Declarator	a court's judgment
Lease	from 1857, long leases (31 years of more) could be recorded
Liferent	right to possess during the grantee's lifetime (applicable especially to widows)
Minute of consolidation	the extinction of a superiority through absorption of the estate with that of the over-superior
Notice of title	inheritance
Postponement, Deed of	extension of a bond
Pr(ecept) (of) Ch(ancery)	inheritance
Pr(ecept) Cl(are) Con(stat)	inheritance
Ren(unciation)	cancellation of a right (usually a bond and disposition in security)
Transl(ation)	when a bond has been assigned from A to B a subsequent transfer to C is a translation
Trust disp(osition)	transfer of a property to another or others as trustee(s)

Other aspects of terminology are explained in law reference texts such as:

BURNS, JOHN, *Hardbook of Conveyancing*, W. Green, 1938.

Of the other records discussed in the chapter, valuation rolls and census enumeration books are to be found in many local history libraries and local record offices. Dean of Guild court records are part of town council archives, whose location is discussed in the notes to Chapter Five. Sheriff court records have been devolved to some of the more established regional record offices, but are under the central authority of the Scottish Record Office, where records for many of the courts remain.

Chapter Three, pp. 50–75

One of the consequences of the chronic housing problem in Scotland has been a considerable literature in this area, which in its turn has attracted the attention of historians.

Predecessors of the Royal Commission on Housing in Scotland 1916 include:

The Royal Commission on the Housing of the Working Classes, 2nd report, Scotland, 1885.

Cost of Living of the Working Classes. Report of an enquiry by the Board of Trade into Working Class Rents, housing and retail prices, 1908.

Glasgow Corporation's Municipal Commission on the Housing of the Poor (established in 1902).

Surveys of the history of housing policy include the following:

CRAMOND, R. D., *Housing Policy in Scotland 1919–1964*, University of Glasgow Research Paper, 1966.

NIVEN, DOUGLAS, *The Development of Housing in Scotland*, Croom Helm, 1979.

PACIONE, M., 'Housing policies in Glasgow since 1880', *Geographical Review*, Volume 69, 4, 1979, pp. 395–412.

Text references to studies of class segregation in housing can be supplemented by:

GAULDIE, ENID, 'The middle class and working class housing', in MACLAREN, A. ALLAN, *Social Class in Scotland Past and Present*, John Donald, n.d. pp. 12–35.

GORDON, G., 'The status areas of early to mid Victorian Edinburgh' *Transactions of the Institute of British Geographers*, New Series 4, 1979, pp. 168–91.

Personal memories of tenement living are recorded in:

FALEY, JEAN, *Up Oor Close: Memories of Domestic Life in Glasgow Tenements 1910–1945*, White Cockade Publishing, 1990.

Public housing is the subject of:

BEGG, TOM, *50 Special Years: A Study in Scottish Housing*, Henry Milland, 1987 (a study of the Scottish Special Housing Association).

MORTON, G. M., *The layout of Glasgow corporation housing schemes 1919–39* (University of Glasgow thesis: Diploma in Town and Regional Planning, 1968).

The architecture of Scottish buildings has also attracted a large literature. A source guide for its study is:

DUNBAR, JOHN G., 'Source materials for the study of Scottish architectural history', *Art Libraries Journal*, Autumn 1979, pp. 17–26.

Sources not mentioned in the text includes Scotland's construction libraries, which are listed in the Construction Industry Information Group directory, architects' offices and the Property Services Agency Regional Office, Scottish Service, Room B110, Argyle House, 3 Lady Lawson Street, Edinburgh EH3 9SD. It is responsible for innumerable plans and photographs of Scotland's public buildings.

A useful guide to architectural terminology is:

PRIDE, GLEN L., *Glossary of Scottish Building*, Famedram, 1975.

Useful periodicals not mentioned in the text are the *Architect* (1869–1926), thereafter united with *Building News* (1855–1926) and *RIBA Transactions/Papers/Journal* (from 1842).

General introductions to Scottish architecture tend not to dwell on the domestic and commercial of the last two hundred years. Useful summaries are:

HAY, GEORGE, *Architecture of Scotland*, Oriel Press, 1969.

MAITLAND, JAMES S., 'Scottish housing past and present', *RIBA Journal*, 1952.

SINCLAIR, FIONA, *Scotstyle: An Examination of the Last 150 Years of Scots Architecture*, RIAS/Scottish Academic Press, 1984. The RIAS/Scottish Academic Press architectural guides mentioned in the text include, apart from those cited (Brogden, 1988, Mckean 1985, Mckean and Walker 1983, 1985, Swan 1987, Walker 1986):

MCKEAN, CHARLES, *Banff and Buchan*, Mainstream, 1990.

MCKEAN, CHARLES, *Central Glasgow*, Mainstream, 1989.

MCKEAN, CHARLES, *District of Moray*, Scottish Academic Press, 1987.

PRIDE, GLEN L., *The Kingdom of Fife: An Illustrated Architectural Guide*, RIAS, 1991.

Another work from the same background is:

MCKEAN, CHARLES, *The Scottish Thirties*, Scottish Academic Press, 1987.

The published 'Pevsner' Penguin guides are as follows:

GIFFORD, JOHN, *Fife*, Penguin, 1988.

GIFFORD, JOHN, MCWILLIAM, COLIN, & WALKER, DAVID, *Edinburgh*, Penguin, 1984.

MCWILLIAM, COLIN, *Lothian except Edinburgh*, Penguin, 1978.

WILLIAMSON, ELIZABETH, RICHES, ANNE & HIGGS, MALCOLM, *Glasgow*, Penguin, 1990.

Other literature on the architecture of specific towns tends to be restricted to the big cities, with next to nothing on the rest:

GOMME, ANDOR & WALKER, DAVID, *The Architecture of Glasgow*, Lund Humphries, 1987.

KERSTING, ANTHONY F., & LINDSAY, MAURICE, *The Buildings of Edinburgh*, Batsford, 1981.

WORSDALL, FRANK, *Victorian City: A Selection of Glasgow Architecture*, Richard Drew, 1982.

Chapter Four, pp. 76–101

The history of shops and shopping in Scotland has not been studied in any depth at all. There is one study of Lipton's:

WAUGH, A., *The Lipton Story*, Cassell, 1951.

Co-operatives have attracted most attention, and there is a bibliography:

SMETHURST, JOHN BLEARS, *A Bibliography of Co-operative Societies' Histories*, Co-operative Union Ltd., [1974].

Items published since that date include:

JONES, R., 'Consumers' co-operation in Victorian Edinburgh: the evolution of a location pattern', *Transactions of the Institute of British Geographers*, New Series 4 (1979) pp. 292–305.

KINLOCH, J. & BUTT, J., *History of the Scottish Co-operative Wholesale Society Limited*, Co-operative Wholesale Society, 1981.

Studies of industry have been far more extensive, and the bibliographical coverage reflects this:

MARWICK, WILLIAM H., 'A bibliography of works on Scottish economic history', *Economic History Review*, Volume 3, No. 1, January 1931, pp. 117–37.

MARWICK, WILLIAM H., 'A bibliography of works on Scottish economic history published during the last twenty years', *Economic History Review*, 2nd series, Volume 4, No. 3, 1952, pp. 376–82.

MARWICK, WILLIAM H., 'A bibliography of works on Scottish economic history 1951–62', *Economic History Review*, 2nd series, Volume 5, No. 16, August 1963, pp. 147–54.

MARWICK, WILLIAM H., 'A bibliography of works on Scottish economic history during the last decade 1963–70', *Essays in Bibliography and Criticism*, Volume 5, No. 67, 1973.

Annual reviews of literature appear in the journals *Scottish Economic and Social History* and *Scottish Industrial History*.

Source guides for the study of business are also numerous:

ARMSTRONG, J. & JONES, J., *Business Documents: Their Origins, Sources and Use to the Historian*, Mansell, 1987.

CAMPBELL, R. H. & DOW, J. B. A., *Source Book of Scottish Economic and Social History*, Blackwell, 1968.

ORBELL, J., *A Guide to Tracing the History of a Business*, Gower, 1987.

Two papers on sources, by John Imrie and A. M. Broom respectively, appear in:

PAYNE, P. L., *Studies in Scottish Business History*, Cass, 1967 (pp. 3–29 and 30–76).

There are also source guides for specific industries, as follows:

COCKERELL, H. A. L., *The British Insurance Business 1547–1970: an introduction and guide to historical records in the United Kingdom*, Heinemann, 1976.

PRESSNELL, L. S. & ORBELL, J., *A Guide to the Historical Records of British Banking*, Gower, 1985.

RITCHIE, L. A., *The Shipbuilding Industry: a guide to historical records*, Manchester University Press, 1990.

RICHMOND, L. M. & TURTON, A., *The Brewing Industry: a guide to historical records*, Manchester University Press, 1989.

Limited liability companies registered in Scotland can be traced through the registers for defunct companies held in the Scottish Record Office. For those registered with the London Stock Exchange there is a published guide: *Register of Defunct Companies*, 2nd edition, Stock Exchange Press: Macmillan, 1990.

The varied literature on Scottish business history can be divided into different categories. General economic histories are numerous and well known, and have been joined in recent years by several works on historical geography (MILLMAN, 1975, TURNOCK 1982, WHITTINGTON & WHYTE 1983). For labour history there is a source guide:

MACDOUGALL, IAN, *A Catalogue of Some Labour Records in Scotland and Some Scots Records outside Scotland*, Scottish Labour History Society, 1978.

The pioneer study of industrial archaeology was:

BUTT, JOHN, *Industrial Archaeology of Scotland*, David & Charles, 1967.

It was followed by a two-volume national survey:

HUME, JOHN R., *Industrial Archaeology of Scotland*, Volume 1, *The Lowlands and Borders*, Batsford, 1976; Volume 2, *The Highlands and Islands*, Batsford, 1977.

Industrial monuments have also been included in the inventory volumes of the Royal Commission on Ancient and Historical Monuments of Scotland that have been published in the last twenty years. A recent large-scale study is:

HAY, GEOFFREY D. & STELL, GEOFFREY P., *Monuments of Industry*, HMSO, 1986.

Regional business studies have become numerous. Examples are:

BUTT, J. & GORDON, G., *Strathclyde: Changing Horizons*, Scottish Academic Press, 1985.

SLAVEN, A., *The Development of the West of Scotland 1750–1960*, Routledge & K. Paul, 1975.

WOOD, SYDNEY, *The Shaping of 19th Century Aberdeenshire*, Spa Books, 1985.

Studies of individual companies vary in quality – many that are sponsored by the firms themselves are under some pressure to avoid controversy.

There are a number of standard surveys of specific industries throughout Scotland, including the following:

BARNARD, A., *The Whisky Distilleries of the United Kingdom*, 1887 (reprinted David & Charles, 1969; Mainstream 1987).

BUTT, J. & PONTING, K., *Scottish Textile History*, Aberdeen University Press, 1987.

CLOW, A. & N., *The Chemical Revolution*, Batchworth Press, 1952.

BREMNER, DAVID, *The Industries of Scotland: Their Rise, Progress and Present Condition*, Black, 1869 (facsimile reprint by David & Charles).

DONNACHIE, IAN, *A History of the Brewing Industry in Scotland*, John Donald, 1979.

DURIE, A. J., *The Scottish Linen Industry in the Eighteenth Century*, John Donald, 1978.

GULVIN, CLIFFORD, *The Scottish Hosiery and Knitwear Industry, 1680–1980*, John Donald, 1984.

MURRAY, NORMAN, *The Scottish Hand Loom Weavers*, John Donald, 1978.

MOSS, M. & HUME, J., *Workshop of the British Empire: Engineering and Shipbuilding in the West of Scotland*, Heinemann, 1977.

The thousands of small limited liability companies resulting from the mid-nineteenth-century legislation are the subject of a fascinating publication:

PAYNE, PETER L., *The Early Scottish Limited Companies 1856–1895: an historical and analytical survey*, Scottish Academic Press, 1980.

Of primary sources for the study of businesses, few have been published, apart from the occasional anthology such as: *Scottish Industrial History*, Scottish History Society, 1978.

One very useful primary source relating to legal processes is sequestration records, especially the Bill Chamber productions (CS96) which include inventories of bankrupts' effects (the Alyth merchant cited on page 79 was a bankrupt, reference CS96 1208 1). West Register House, where the records are held has an *Alphabetical list of sequestrated bankrupts 1839–1913*. The 'productions' (any documentary or other physical evidence brought to the court) are inventoried in *Scottish Record Office, Court of Session Productions c. 1760–1840*, List & Index Society, Special series Volume 23, 1987.

The relationship between the local economy and modern business development continues to fascinate, and the local historian can bring the story up to date in various studies, including:

HOOD, NEIL & YOUNG, STEPHEN, *Multinationals in Retreat: The Scottish Experience*, Edinburgh University Press, 1982.

KEATING, MICHAEL & BOYLE, ROBIN, *Remaking Urban Scotland: Strategies for Local Economic Development*, Edinburgh University Press, 1986.

Chapter Five, pp. 102–34

The history of urban local government from early times is the subject of: MURRAY, DAVID, *Early Burgh Organisation in Scotland*, Jackson Wylie, 1932 (2 volumes).

For recent times, there is no standard work, and the sometimes confusing administrative background can only be traced through handbooks of administrative law published at key points in its development. The following are useful:

MCLARTY, M. R., *Source Book and History of Administrative Law in Scotland*, Hodge, 1956.

MILLER, J. BENNETT, *An Outline of Administrative and Local Government Law in Scotland*, W. Green, 1961.

WHYTE, W. E., *Local Government in Scotland*, Hodge, 1925 (a second edition, 1936, shows all the changes of the major 1929 Local Government (Scotland) Act.) There are also important studies of specific aspects of administrative law, for example poor law. Bibliographical coverage of many of these is contained in:

MAXWELL, LESLIE F. & W. H., *Scottish Law to 1956*, Volume 5 of *A Legal Bibliography of the British Commonwealth of Nations*, 2nd edition, Sweet & Maxwell, 1957.

Sources for public services

harbours and ports – originally controlled by burgh councils, some of the more important were transferred into the hands of commissioners in the nineteenth century. Management of the smaller harbours remains in local council control. The Exchequer records in the Scottish Record Office include customs accounts from the seventeenth to nineteenth centuries. Independent growth in the nineteenth century was linked to the development of fishing (Fishery Board archives within Scottish Office records) and railways (British Rail archives in the Scottish Record Office). After 1948, railway docks were administered by the British Transport Commission and its successors (now British Transport Dock Board).

health and social services – most of Scotland's health boards have set up their own archive centres which hold a variety of records supplementing those in local record offices and the Scottish Office records.

A fascinating introduction to nineteenth-century urban social provision is:

CHECKLAND, OLIVE, *Philanthropy in Victorian Scotland*, John Donald, 1980.

The same period is covered in the densely written:

FERGUSON, THOMAS, *Scottish Social Welfare 1864–1914*, E. & S. Livingstone, 1958.

Important recent studies include:

LEVITT, IAN, *Poverty and Welfare in Scotland 1890–1948*, Edinburgh University Press, 1988.

MCLACHLAN, GORDON, *Improving the Common Weal: Aspects of Scottish Health Services 1900–1984*, Edinburgh University Press, 1987.

police – police responsibility has remained a *quasi* local government function since the time of the first burgh police acts (1833). The main change has been the progressive consolidation of responsibility within the hands of fewer and fewer authorities. The process began with the Police (Scotland) Act 1857 which made county police forces obligatory under the supervision of the commissioners of supply, and allowed burghs to consolidate their forces with the former. The Local Government (Scotland) Act 1889 obliged all burghs with populations under 7,000 (except Renfrew and Lerwick) to relinquish control. The 1929 Local Government (Scotland) Act increased the population figure to 20,000, and the Police (Scotland) Act 1956 allowed for amalgamations of county forces.

railways – as with other utilities (roads, harbours, water) there are numerous plans deposited with sheriff courts which are now in the plan collection of West Register House. Records of the private railway companies were taken over by British Railways at nationalization.

roads and bridges – the first major consolidating act was the Roads and Bridges (Scotland) Act 1878 which abolished turnpike roads and put most powers into the hands of commissioners of supply and burgh councils. The post-1889 county councils administered the former's roads through district committees with representatives from parochial boards and each burgh. In 1929 all classified roads in small burghs were transferred to county councils. Records are held by regional councils.

schools – the Scottish Council for Research in Education, 15 St John Street, Edinburgh, has published numerous volumes on aspects of the history of Scottish schooling. A more recent establishment is the History of Education Centre, London Street School, East London Street, Edinburgh. Bibliographical coverage is also good:

CRAIGIE, JAMES, *A Bibliography of Scottish Education before 1872*, University of London Press, 1970.

CRAIGIE, JAMES, *A Bibliography of Scottish Education 1872–1972*, University of London Press, 1974.

SCOTLAND, JAMES, *History of Scottish Education*, 2 volumes, University of London Press, 1969 (contains substantial bibliography).

town planning – a general introductory guide is:

ASHWORTH, WILLIAM, *The Genesis of Modern British Town Planning*, Routledge & Kegan Paul, 1954.

The Planning Exchange, founded in Glasgow in 1972, brings together professionals, academics and politicians interested in problems and research.

water supply and sewage – the only general introductory text to the subject is:

ROBINS, F. W., *The Story of Water Supply*, Oxford University Press, 1949.

General powers for local authorities to provide water were consolidated in the Waterworks Clauses Acts 1847 and 1863. The Public Health (Scotland) Act 1867 complicated the situation by allowing the establishment of special districts for water supply schemes where the local residents so wished. Though special districts (also later set up for lighting and refuse collection) were seen mainly as a solution for villages, some were wholly or partly within burghs. They lasted until the reforms of 1974, though not after the Water (Scotland) Act 1949 for water supply.

A more detailed analysis of the history of local government functions forms an appendix to MOODY (1986) and is treated comprehensively in MCLARTY, cited on page 152.

A new two-volume work on nineteenth-century burgh legislation is:

URQUHART, RODERICK M., *The Burghs of Scotland and the Burgh Police (Scotland) Act 1833*, Scottish Library Association, 1991.

URQUHART, RODERICK M., *The Burghs of Scotland and the Burgh Police and the Policing of Towns (Scotland) Act 1850*, Scottish Library Association, 1991.

The politics of local government has received equally sparse treatment, apart from:

HUTCHINSON, I. G. C., *A Political History of Scotland 1832–1924*, John Donald, 1985.

Nineteenth-century church buildings can be studied in two journals, the *Ecclesiologist* 1842–68 and the *Church Builder* 1862–1904. Most church denominations have their own histories. Church of Scotland records, plus those of secessions subsequently reunited, are held in the Scottish Record Office, as are records of the Episcopal church, Methodists and Quakers. The most useful local records of each parish church are the kirk session minute books. Collections of church magazines are frequently found in local history library ephemera and help to provide a picture of urban pastoralism. Cemeteries (including those which were once churchyards) are the responsibility of district councils, who often hold burial registers and other records in their archives, or with their birth, marriage and death registration officers. As parish councils and the old district councils also at different times controlled sites, their archives (held with county council records) can also be fruitful.

Burgh records

Some burghs have council records dating back to the sixteenth century, and even before in one or two cases. The core records are the town council minute books, of which most early survivals have been published in book form. Closely associated in early times are the records of the guilds. None of the latter are extant from before the fifteenth century, even though by 1400 at least 19 burghs had a guild or at least the right to possess one. The majority of royal burghs had adopted guilds or merchants' associations in the century after 1560; and alongside these had grown up lesser associations of craftsmen known as incorporations. Each trade – fleshers, cordiners, hammermen and so on – had its own incorporation and set of minute books. A second group of burgh records is the accounts, kept under charge (income) and discharge (expenditure). Published abstracts of accounts have continued up to the present. A third group of long-standing records are court archives, both the Dean of Guild court discussed in the text and the Burgh Court, whose powers had been severely truncated before the time of surviving records. Today's District Court is its linear successor.

Location of burgh records

With the demise of Scottish burghs in 1974/5, their records have been inherited by the post-1974 District Councils. However, the current arrangement in any locality has usually depended upon agreements with other bodies, such as regional councils and universities, to find common accommodation of good quality for archival storage. Pre-nineteenth-century records of royal burghs, being particularly precious, are in many cases deposited with the Scottish Record Office. This is certainly the case with the main legal records, such as the registers of deeds, the burgh registers of sasines, and their predecessors the protocol books.

The list which follows is based upon a detailed card index kept in the West Register House of the Scottish Record Office.

Burgh	Location
Aberchirder	*see* Banff
Aberdeen	Aberdeen District Archives, Town House, Aberdeen
Aberfeldy	Sandeman Library, Kinnoull Street, Perth
Aberlour	Moray District Record Office, Tollbooth, Forres
Abernethy	Sandeman Library, Kinnoull Street, Perth
Airdrie	Monklands District Council, Municipal Buildings, Dunbeth Road, Coatbridge
Alloa	Central Regional Archives, Spittal Street, Stirling

Alva	Central Regional Archives, Spittal Street, Stirling
Alyth	Sandeman Library, Kinnoull Street, Perth
Annan	District Council Office, High Street, Annan
Anstruther	*see* Kilrenny
Arbroath	Montrose Public Library, High Street, Montrose
Ardrossan	Cunninghame Library Headquarters, Princes Street, Ardrossan
Armadale	West Lothian District Library Headquarters, Wellpark, Bathgate
Auchterarder	Sandeman Library, Kinnoull Street, Perth
Auchtermuchty	St Andrews University Archives
Ayr	Carnegie Library, Main Street, Ayr
Ballater	Kincardine & Deeside District Council, Arduthie Road, Stonehaven
Banchory	Kincardine & Deeside District Council, local office, Banchory
Banff	Banff & Buchan District Council, Sandyhill Road, Banff (some records in Grampian Regional Archive)
Barrhead	Renfrew District Council, Collier Street, Johnstone
Bathgate	West Lothian District Library Headquarters, Wellpark, Bathgate
Bearsden	Bearsden District Council, Boclair, Milngavie Road, Bearsden
Biggar	Clydesdale District Council Offices, Lanark
Bishopbriggs	Strathkelvin District Council Chambers, Kirkintilloch
Blairgowrie & Rattray	Sandeman Library, Kinnoull Street, Perth
Bo'ness	Central Regional Archives, Spittal Street, Stirling
Bonnyrigg & Lasswade	Edinburgh City Archives, City Chambers, High Street, Edinburgh
Brechin	Montrose Public Library, High Street, Montrose

Bridge of Allan	Central Regional Archives, Spittal Street, Stirling
Buckhaven & Methil	Kirkcaldy District Council Office, Town House, Kirkcaldy
Buckie	Moray District Record Office, Tollbooth, Forres
Burghead	Moray District Record Office, Tollbooth, Forres
Burntisland	Scottish Record Office/Kirkcaldy District Council Office/Information Office, Kirkgate, Burntisland
Callander	Central Regional Archives, Spittal Street, Stirling
Campbeltown	Argyll & Bute District Council, Archivist, Kilmory, Lochgilphead
Carnoustie	Montrose Public Library, High Street, Montrose
Castle Douglas	Stewartry District Council, Council Offices, Kirkcudbright
Clydebank	Clydebank Public Library, Dumbarton Road, Clydebank
Coatbridge	Monklands District Council, Municipal Buildings, Dunbeth Road, Monklands
Cockenzie & Port Seton	Scottish Record Office
Coldstream	Berwickshire District Council Office, Newton Street, Duns
Coupar Angus	Sandeman Library, Kinnoull Street, Perth
Cove & Kilcreggan	Dumbarton District Council, Crosslet House, Dumbarton
Cowdenbeath	Dunfermline District Council, City Chambers, Dunfermline
Crail	Scottish Record Office/St Andrews University Archives
Crieff	Sandeman Library, Kinnoull Street, Perth
Cromarty	Dingwall District Council Buildings, Dingwall
Cumnock & Holmhead	Cumnock & Doon Valley Council Offices, Lugar, Cumnock
Cullen	Moray District Record Office, Tollbooth, Forres

Culross	Scottish Record Office/Dunfermline District Council, City Chambers, Dunfermline
Cumbernauld	Cumbernauld District Council, Bron Way, Cumbernauld
Cupar	Scottish Record Office/St Andrews University Archives
Dalbeattie	Stewartry District Council Offices, Kirkcudbright
Dalkeith	Edinburgh City Archives, City Chambers, High Street, Edinburgh
Darvel	Kilmarnock & Loudon District Council, Civic Centre, Kilmarnock
Denny & Dunipace	Central Regional Archives, Spittal Street, Stirling
Dingwall	Scottish Record Office/Dingwall Museum
Dollar	Central Regional Archives, Spittal Street, Stirling
Dornoch	District Council Offices, Golspie/ Inverness Public Library, Farraline Park, Inverness
Doune	Central Regional Archives, Spittal Street, Stirling
Dufftown	Moray District Record Office, Tollbooth, Forres
Dumbarton	Dumbarton District Library, Helenslee Road, Dumbarton
Dumfries	Nithsdale District Council Municipal Chambers, Dumfries
Dunbar	Scottish Record Office
Dunblane	Central Regional Archives, Spittal Street, Stirling
Dundee	Dundee Archive and Record Centre, 14 City Square, Dundee
Dunfermline	District Council Office, City Chambers, Dunfermline
Dunoon	Argyll & Bute District Council, Archivist, Kilmory, Lochgilphead
Duns	Berwickshire District Council Office, Newton Street, Duns
Dysart	Kirkcaldy District Council Office, Town House, Kirkcaldy

East Kilbride	Council Office, Civic Centre, East Kilbride/Haig Building, Markinch
East Linton	Scottish Record Office
Edinburgh	City Chambers, High Street, Edinburgh
Elgin	Moray District Record Office, Tollbooth, Forres
Elie & Earlsferry	Scottish Record Office/St Andrews University Archives
Ellon	Grampian Regional Council Archives, Dunbar Street, Aberdeen
Eyemouth	District Council Offices, Eyemouth and Duns
Falkirk	Central Regional Archives, Spittal Street, Stirling
Falkland	St Andrews University Archives
Findochty	Moray District Record Office, Tollbooth, Forres
Forfar	Montrose Public Library, High Street, Montrose
Fort William	Public Library, Farraline Park, Inverness/Lochaber District Council, Lochaber House
Fortrose	Scottish Record Office/Locality Office, Fortrose
Fraserburgh	Grampian Regional Council Archives, Dunbar Street, Aberdeen
Galashiels	Ettrick & Lauderdale District Council, Paton Street, Galashiels
Galston	Kilmarnock Civic Centre, Kilmarnock
Gatehouse of Fleet	Stewartry District Council Offices, Kirkcudbright
Girvan	Carnegie Library, Main Street, Ayr
Glasgow	Strathclyde Regional Archives, Mitchell Library, Glasgow
Glenrothes	Haig Building, Markinch
Gourock	James Watt Institute, Greenock
Grangemouth	Central Regional Archives, Spittal Street, Stirling
Grantown on Spey	Badenoch & Strathspey Council Office, Ruthven Road, Kingussie
Greenock	Municipal Buildings, Greenock/James Watt Institute, Greenock
Haddington	Scottish Record Office

Hamilton	Hamilton Public Library, Cadzow Street, Hamilton
Hawick	Roxburgh District Council, High Street, Hawick
Helensburgh	Dumbarton District Library, Helenslee Road, Dumbarton
Huntley	Grampian Regional Archives, Dunbar Street, Aberdeen
Innerleithen	Tweeddale District Council Office, Rosetta Road, Peebles
Inveraray	Arygll & Bute District Council, Archivist, Kilmory, Lochgilphead
Inverbervie	Kincardine & Deeside District Council, Arduthie Road, Stonehaven
Invergordon	Council Offices, Dingwall
Inverkeithing	Scottish Record Office/Inverkeithing Burgh Museum/Dunfermline District Council, City Chambers, Dunfermline
Inverness	Town House, Inverness/Public Library, Farraline Park, Inverness
Inverurie	Grampian Regional Council Archives, Dunbar Street, Aberdeen
Irvine	Scottish Record Office/Irvine Burns Club/Library Headquarters, Ardrossan/Legal Library, Cunninghame House
Jedburgh	Roxburgh District Council, High Street, Hawick
Johnstone	Renfrew District Council, Collier Street, Johnstone
Keith	Moray District Record Office, Tollbooth, Forres
Kelso	Roxburgh District Council, High Street, Hawick
Kilmarnock	Civic Centre, Kilmarnock
Kilrenny, Anstruther East & West	Scottish Record Office/St Andrews University Archives
Kilsyth	Kilsyth Local Office, Parkfoot Street, Kilsyth
Kilwinning	Library Headquarters, Princes Street, Ardrossan

Kinghorn	District Council Office, Town House, Kirkcaldy
Kingussie	Badenoch & Strathspey District Council Office, High Street, Kingussie
Kinross	Sandeman Library, Kinnoull Street, Perth
Kintore	Scottish Record Office/Grampian Regional Council Archives, Dunbar Street, Aberdeen
Kirkcaldy	District Council Office, Town House, Kirkcaldy
Kirkcudbright	Town Hall, Kirkcudbright/Stewartry District Council Office, Kirkcudbright
Kirkintilloch	William Patrick Library, Kirkintilloch
Kirkwall	Public Library, Laing Street, Kirkwall
Kirriemuir	Montrose Public Library, High Street, Montrose
Ladybank	St Andrews University Archives
Lanark	Clydesdale District Council Office, Lanark
Langholm	Local Government Office, Langholm
Largs	Library Headquarters, Princes Street, Ardrossan
Lauder	Scottish Record Office/Ettrick & Lauderdale District Council, Paton Street, Galashiels
Laurencekirk	Kincardine & Deeside District Council, Arduthie Road, Stonehaven
Lerwick	Shetland Archive, King Harald Street, Lerwick
Leslie	Kirkcaldy District Council Office, Town House, Kirkcaldy
Leven	Carberry House, Leven/Kirkcaldy District Council Office, Town House, Kirkcaldy
Linlithgow	Scottish Record Office/West Lothian District Library, Wellpark, Bathgate
Loanhead	Edinburgh City Archive, City Chambers, High Street, Edinburgh
Lochgelly	Dunfermline District Council, City Chambers, Dunfermline

Lochgilphead	Argyll & Bute District Council, Archivist, Kilmory, Lochgilphead
Lochmaben	Scottish Record Office/Local Government Office, Lochmaben
Lockerbie	Local Government Office, Lockerbie
Lossiemouth	Moray District Record Office, Tollbooth, Forres
Macduff	Grampian Regional Council Archives, Dunbar Street, Aberdeen
Markinch	Kirkcaldy District Council Office, Town House, Kirkcaldy
Maybole	Carnegie Library, Main Street, Ayr
Melrose	Ettrick & Lauderdale District Council, Paton Street, Galashiels
Millport	Library headquarters, Princes Street, Ardrossan
Milngavie	Bearsden District Council Office, Boclair, Milngavie Road, Bearsden
Moffat	Local Government Office, Moffat
Monifieth	Dundee Archive and Record Centre, 14 City Square, Dundee
Montrose	Montrose Public Library, High Street, Montrose
Motherwell & Wishaw	Civic Centre, Motherwell
Musselburgh	Scottish Record Office
New Galloway	Stewartry District Council Office, Kirkcudbright
Newmilns & Greenholm	Civic Centre, Kilmarnock
Newport on Tay	St Andrews University Archives
Newton Stewart	Wigtown District Council Office, Stranraer
North Berwick	Scottish Record Office
Oban	Argyll & Bute District Council, Archivist, Kilmory, Lochgilphead
Old Meldrum	Grampian Regional Council Archives, Dunbar Street, Aberdeen
Paisley	Renfrew District Council, Collier Street, Johnstone
Peebles	District Council Office, Rosetta Road, Peebles
Penicuik	Edinburgh City Archives, City Chambers, High St, Edinburgh

Perth	Sandeman Library, Kinnoull Street, Perth
Peterhead	Grampian Regional Council Archives, Dunbar Street, Aberdeen
Pitlochry	Sandeman Library, Kinnoull Street, Perth
Pittenweem	St Andrews University Archives
Port Glasgow	Watt Library, Greenock
Portknockie	Moray District Record Office, Tollbooth, Forres
Portsoy	see Banff
Prestonpans	Scottish Record Office
Prestwick	Carnegie Library, Main Street, Ayr
Queensferry	Edinburgh City Archives, City Chambers, High Street, Edinburgh
Renfrew	Renfrew District Council, Collier Street, Johnstone
Rosehearty	Grampian Regional Archives, Dunbar Street, Aberdeen
Rothes	Moray District Record Office, Tollbooth, Forres
Rothesay	Argyll & Bute District Council, Archivist, Kilmory, Lochgilphead
Rutherglen	Strathclyde Regional Archives, Mitchell Library, Glasgow
St Monance	St Andrews University Archives
Saltcoats	Library Headquarters, Princes Street, Ardrossan
Sanquhar	Scottish Record Office/Council Chambers, High Street, Sanquhar
Selkirk	Ettrick & Lauderdale District Council, Paton Street, Galashiels
Stevenston	Library Headquarters, Princes Street, Ardrossan
St Andrews	St Andrews University Archives
Stewarton	Civic Centre, Kilmarnock
Stirling	Central Regional Archives, Spittal Street, Stirling
Stonehaven	Kincardine & Deeside District Council, Arduthie Road, Stonehaven
Stornoway	Stornoway Town Hall, Sandwick Road, Stornoway
Stranraer	District Council Office, Stranraer

Stromness	Public Library, Kirkwall
Tain	Scottish Record Office/Locality Office, Tain/Council Buildings, Dingwall
Tayport	St Andrews University Archives
Thurso	District Council Office, Wick/Locality Office, Thurso
Tillicoultry	Central Regional Archives, Spittal Street, Stirling
Tobermory	Argyll & Bute District Council, Archivist, Kilmory, Lochgilphead
Tranent	Scottish Record Office
Troon	Carnegie Library, Main Street, Ayr
Turriff	Grampian Regional Archives, Dunbar Street, Aberdeen
Whitburn	West Lothian District Library, Wellpark, Bathgate
Whithorn	District Council Office, Stranraer
Wick	District Council Office, Wick/Town Hall, Wick
Wigtown	District Council Office, Stranraer

Location of County Council Records

Aberdeen	Grampian Regional Archives, Dunbar Street, Aberdeen
Angus	per Montrose Public Library, High Street, Montrose
Argyll	Argyll & Bute District Council, Archivist, Kilmory, Lochgilphead
Ayr	Strathclyde Regional Council, Local Office, Wellington Square, Ayr
Banff	Moray District Record Office, Tollbooth, Forres
Berwick	Duns Public Library, Newton Street, Duns
Bute	Strathclyde Regional Archives, Mitchell Library, Glasgow
Caithness	Public Library, Farraline Park, Inverness
Clackmannan	Central Regional Archives, Spittal Street, Stirling
Dumfries	Ewart Library, Dumfries

Dunbarton	Strathclyde Regional Archives, Mitchell Library, Glasgow
East Lothian	Scottish Record Office
Fife	Archive, West Wemyssfield/Educational Resource Centre, Kirkcaldy
Kincardine	Grampian Regional Archives, Dunbar Street, Aberdeen
Inverness	Public Library, Farraline Park, Inverness
Kinross	Sandeman Public Library, Kinnoull Street, Perth
Kirkcudbright	Ewart Library, Dumfries
Lanark	Strathclyde Regional Archives, Mitchell Library, Glasgow
Midlothian	Scottish Record Office/Library Headquarters, Roslin/St Giles Sub Basement, High Street, Edinburgh
Moray & Nairn	Moray District Record Office, Tollbooth, Forres/Public Library, Farraline Park, Inverness
Nairn	Court House, Nairn
Orkney	Orkney Library, Laing Street, Kirkwall
Peebles	Borders Region Library Headquarters, Newtown St Boswells
Perth	Sandeman Library, Kinnoull Street, Perth
Renfrew	Strathclyde Regional Archives, Mitchell Library, Glasgow
Ross & Cromarty	Public Library, Farraline Park, Inverness/Council Buildings, Stornoway/Library, Stornoway
Roxburgh	Borders Region Library Headquarters, Newtown St Boswells
Selkirk	Borders Region Library Headquarters, Newtown St Boswells
Stirling	Central Regional Archives, Spittal Street, Stirling
Sutherland	Public Library, Farraline Park, Inverness
West Lothian	West Lothian District Library, Wellpark, Bathgate
Wigtown	Ewart Library, Dumfries

Zetland   Shetland Archive, King Harald Street,
                           Lerwick

REFERENCES

ADAMS, IAN H. (1978), *The Making of Urban Scotland*, Croom Helm

ALDCROFT, DEREK H. (1982), 'Urban transport problems in historical perspective', *in* SLAVEN and ALDCROFT (1982) pp. 220–32

BARRETT, HELENA and PHILLIPS, JOHN (1987), *Suburban Style: The British Home 1840–1960*, Macdonald Orbis

BEST, G. F. A. (1968), 'The Scottish Victorian city', *Victorian Studies* XI, March 1968, pp. 329–57

BEST G. F. A. (1973), 'Another part of the island: some Scottish perspectives', *in* DYOS and WOLFF (1973) pp. 389–411

BRICE, MARTIN H. (1984), *Stronghold: A History of Military Architecture*, Batsford

BRIGGS, ASA (1968), 'Forward', *in* DYOS, H. J. (1968)

BROGDEN, W. A. (1988), *Aberdeen: An Illustrated Architectural Guide*, 2nd edition, Scottish Academic Press/RIAS

BURNETT, JOHN (1978), *A Social History of Housing 1815–1970*, David & Charles

BURT, EDWARD (1722), *Letters from a Gentleman in the North of Scotland*

BYATT, ANTHONY (1978), *Picture Postcards and Their Publishers: An Illustrated Account. . .*, Golden Age Postcard Books

CHADWICK, G. F. (1966), *The Park and the Town: Public Landscape in the 19th and 20th Centuries*, Architectural Press

CHECKLAND, S. G. (1975), *Scottish Banking: A History 1695–1973*, Collins

CHECKLAND, S. G. (1976), *The Upas Tree: Glasgow 1875–1975*, University of Glasgow Press

CONZEN, M. R. G. (1968), 'The use of town plans in the study of urban history', *in* DYOS (1968) pp. 113–30

CRAIG THOMAS (1934), *The Jus Feudale*, translated by James Avon Clyde, Hodge

CURL, JAMES STEVENS (1972), *The Victorian Celebration of Death*, David & Charles

DAUNTON, M. J. (1983), 'Public place and private space', *in* FRASER & SUTCLIFFE (1983)

DAVIS, DOROTHY (1966), *History of Shopping*, Routledge & Kegan Paul

DEAN, DAVID (1970), *English Shop Fronts from Contemporary Source Books 1792–1840*, Alec Tiranti

DENEKE, DIETRICH and SHAW, GARETH (1988), *Urban Historical Geography: Recent Progress in Britain and Germany*, Cambridge University Press

DICKS, BRIAN (1985), 'Choice and constraint: further perspectives on socio-residential segregation in nineteenth-century Glasgow with particular reference to its West End', *in* GORDON (1985) pp. 91–124

DOHERTY, J. (1983), 'Urbanization, capital accumulation and class struggle in Scotland 1750–1914', *in* WHITTINGTON & WHYTE (1983) pp. 239–67

DONNACHIE, IAN and MACLEOD, INNES (1979), *Victorian and Edwardian Scottish Lowlands from Historic Photographs*, Batsford

DYOS, H. J. (1968) *The Study of Urban History*, Edward Arnold

DYOS, H. J. and WOLFF, MICHAEL (1973), *Victorian City: Images and Realities*, 2 volumes, Routledge & Kegan Paul

EASTLAKE, CHARLES L. (1978), *A History of the Gothic Revival*, Leicester University Press (reprint of 1872 edition)

ELLIOT, B. and MCCRONE, D. (1980), 'Urban development in Edinburgh: a contribution to the political economy of place', *Scottish Journal of Sociology*, 4(1) January 1980, pp. 1–26

FLINN, M. (1977), *Scottish Population History*, Cambridge University Press

FORSYTH, W. (1982), 'Urban economic morphology in nineteenth-century Glasgow', *in* SLAVEN & ALDCROFT (1982) pp. 166–92

FRASER, DEREK and SUTCLIFFE, ANTHONY (1983), *The Pursuit of Urban History*, Edward Arnold

FRASER, HAMISH (1985), 'Labour and the changing city', *in* GORDON (1985) pp. 160–79

GORDON, GEORGE (1985), *Perspectives of the Scottish city*, Aberdeen University Press

HART, TOM (1982), 'Urban growth and municipal government: Glasgow in a comparative context 1846–1914', *in* SLAVEN & ALDCROFT (1982) pp. 193–219

HEDBERG, ANDERS (1945), Article by Mr Anders Hedberg, Swedish Co-operative Union, on his visit to East Lothian Co-operative Society Ltd in 1945, translated by Mr John Downie, Wishaw (typescript)

HERBERT, DAVID T. and THOMAS, COLIN J. (1982), *Urban Geography: A First Approach*, John Wiley & Sons

HIGGS, LESLIE (1977), *New Towns: Social Involvement in Livingston*, Maclellan

JEFFERYS, JAMES B. (1954), *Retail Trading in Britain 1850–1950*, Cambridge University Press

JONES, FRANCIS M. (1968), 'The aesthetic of the nineteenth century industrial town', *in* DYOS (1968) pp. 171–82

JORDAN, ROBERT F. (1966), *Victorian Architecture*, Penguin

KEITH, A. (1972), *A Thousand Years of Aberdeen*, Aberdeen University Press

KING, ANTHONY J. (1984), *The Bungalow: The Production of a Global Culture*, Routledge & Kegan Paul

LEVITT, IAN (1988), *Government and Social Conditions in Scotland, 1845–1919*, Scottish History Society

LINDSAY, MAURICE (1987), *Victorian and Edwardian Glasgow from Old Photographs*, Batsford

LYNCH, MICHAEL, SPEARMAN, MICHAEL and STELL, GEOFFREY (1988), *The Scottish Medieval Town*, John Donald

MCKAY, JOHN H. (1988), 'Retail co-operatives in the shale mining areas of the Almond valley 1872–1914', *in A Sense of Place: Studies in Scottish Local History*, Scotland's Cultural Heritage

MCKEAN, CHARLES (1985), *Stirling and the Trossachs*, RIAS/Scottish Academic Press

MCKEAN, CHARLES (1988), 'Standing the test of time and style', *Scotland on Sunday*, 4 September 1988, p. 45

MCKEAN, CHARLES and WALKER, DAVID (1983), *Edinburgh: An Illustrated Architectural Guide*, 3rd edition, RIAS/Scottish Academic Press

MCKEAN, CHARLES and WALKER, DAVID (1985), *Dundee: An Illustrated Introduction*, 2nd edition, RIAS/Scottish Academic Press

MCKICHAN, FINLAY (1978), 'A burgh's response to the problems of urban growth: Stirling 1780–1880', *Scottish History Review* 57, 1978, pp. 68–86

MCWILLIAM, COLIN (1975), *Scottish Townscape*, Collins

MAIR, CRAIG (1988), *Mercat Cross and Tolbooth: Understanding Scotland's Old Burghs*, John Donald

MAJOR, J. KENNETH (1975), *Fieldwork in Industrial Archaeology*, Batsford

MARCUS, STEVEN (1973), 'Reading the illegible', *in* DYOS & WOLFF (1973), Volume 1, pp. 257–76

MARSHALL, NESSIE (1984), *A Pennyworth o' Elephants' Tiptaes: A Century of Selkirk's Shops*, Ettrick & Lauderdale District Council Museum Service

MARTIN, G. H. (1968), 'The town as palimpsest', *in* DYOS (1968) pp. 155–69

MILLMAN, R. N. (1975), *The Making of the Scottish Landscape*, Batsford

MONTEATH, H. H. (1958), 'Heritable rights: from early times to the twentieth century', in *Introduction to Scottish Legal History*, Stair Society, 1958, pp. 156–98

MORRIS, R. J. (1983), 'The middle class and the industrial revolution', *in* FRASER & SUTCLIFFE (1983), pp. 286–306

MOZLEY, ANITA VENTURA (1977), *Photographs of the Old Closes and Streets of Glasgow 1868/1877 . . . with a new introduction by Anita Ventura Mozley*, Dover

MUMFORD, LEWIS (1966), *The City in History*, Penguin

NAISMITH, ROBERT J. (1989), *The Story of Scotland's Towns*, John Donald

NENADIC, STANA (1988), 'The rise of the urban middle class', *in* DEVINE, T. M. & MITCHISON, ROSALIND, *People and Society in Scotland I, 1760–1830*, John Donald, pp. 109–26

OLSEN, DONALD J. (1983), 'The city as a work of art', *in* FRASER & SUTCLIFFE (1983), pp. 264–85

ROBERTS, CHRIS and WALLACE, VERONICA (1989), *Edwardian East Lothian*, East Lothian District Library

RODGER, R. G. (1975), *Scottish urban housebuilding 1870–1914* (Edinburgh University PhD)

RODGER, R. G. (1979), 'Speculative builders and the structure of the Scottish building industry 1860–1914', *Business History XXI*, 1979, pp. 226–46

RODGER, R. G. (1983), 'The invisible hand: market forces, housing and the urban form in Victorian cities', *in* FRASER & SUTCLIFFE (1983) pp. 190–211

SAUNDERS, LAURENCE J. (1950), *Scottish Democracy 1815–1840*, Oliver and Boyd

SCHNORE, LEO F. (1968), 'Problems in the quantitative study of urban history', *in* DYOS (1968) pp. 189–208

SCHOENWALD, RICHARD L. (1973), 'Training urban man', *in* DYOS & WOLFF (1973) pp. 669–92

SHAW, GARETH (1988), 'Recent research on the commercial structure of nineteenth-century British cities', *in* DENEKE & SHAW (1988) pp. 236–49

SHAW, G. and WILD, M. T. (1979), 'Retail patterns in the

Victorian city', *Transactions Institute of British Geographers*, new series 4, 1979, pp. 278–91

SIMMONS, JACK (1973), 'The power of the railways', *in* DYOS & WOLFF (1973) pp. 277–310

SIMPSON, M. A. (1977), 'The West End of Glasgow 1830–1914', *in* SIMPSON, M. A. & LLOYD, T. H. *Middle Class Housing in Britain*, David and Charles

SLAVEN, ANTHONY and ALDCROFT, DEREK H. (1982), *Business, Banking and Urban History*, John Donald

SPEARMAN, R. M. (1988), 'Workshops, materials and debris – evidence of early industries', *in* LYNCH, MICHAEL, etc. (1988), pp. 134–47

STAVE, BRUCE (1983), 'A view from the United States', *in* FRASER & SUTCLIFFE (1983)

[SUMMARY] (1918), *Summary of the Report by the Royal Commission on Housing in Scotland*, edited by Archibald Stalker, W. & R. Chambers

SWAN, ADAM (1987), *Clackmannan and the Ochils: An Illustrated Architectural Guide*, RIAS/Scottish Academic Press

TAYLOR, NICHOLAS (1973), 'The awful sublimity of the Victorian city: its aesthetic and architectural origins', *in* DYOS & WOLFF (1973) pp. 431–47

TAYLOR, ROGER (1981), *George Washington Wilson: Artist and Photographer 1823–93*, Aberdeen University Press

THOMPSON, PAUL (1973), 'Voices from within' *in* DYOS & WOLFF (1973) pp. 59–82

TIVY, JOY (1961), 'Four small Scottish burghs', *Scottish Geographical Magazine*, Volume 77, 1961, pp. 148–64

TURNER, STANLEY H. (1908), *The History of Local Taxation in Scotland*, Blackwood

TURNOCK, DAVID (1982), *The Historical Geography of Scotland since 1707*, Cambridge University Press

WALKER, FRANK (1985), 'National romanticism and the architecture of the city', *in* GORDON (1985) pp. 125–59

WALKER, FRANK ARNEIL (1986), *The South Clyde Estuary: An Illustrated Architectural Guide to Inverclyde and Renfrew*, RIAS/Scottish Academic Press

WARD, PAMELA (1968), *Conservation and Development*, Oriel

WARNER, SAM BASS JR (1983), 'The management of multiple urban images', *in* FRASER & SUTCLIFFE (1983)

WHITTINGTON, G. and WHYTE, I. D. (1983), *An Historical Geography of Scotland*, Academic Press

WILSON, DEREK (1985), *Francis Frith's Travels*, J. M. Dent

WORSDALL, FRANK (1979), *The Tenement: A Way of Life*, Chambers

WYNESS, FENTON (1971), *Aberdeen: Century of Change*, Impulse Books

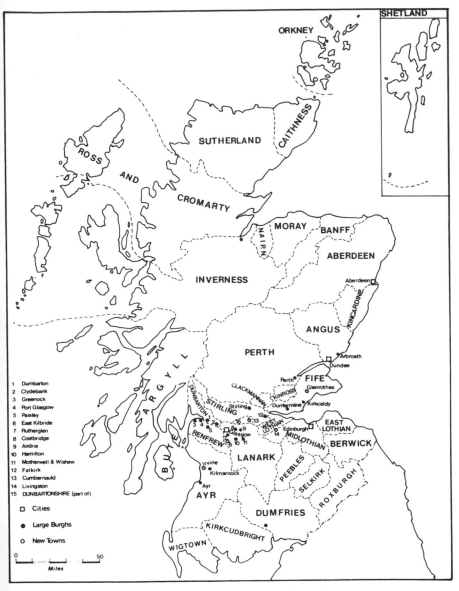

Map of Scotland showing former counties, large burghs and new towns.

INDEX

BOOKS ON LOCAL HISTORY FROM BATSFORD:

Batsford Companion to Local History
Stephen Friar
0 7134 6181 0

Exploring Urban History
Stephen Porter
0 7134 5138 6

Farming: Sources for Local Historians
Peter Edwards
0 7134 5117 3

Folklore of the Scottish Highlands
Anne Ross
0 7134 5447 4

Historic Farm Buildings
Susanna Wade-Martins
0 7134 6507 7

History of Britain: An Aerial View
Christopher Stanley
0 7134 4200 X

Local History: A Handbook for Beginners
Philip Riden
0 7134 3871 1

Maps and Plans for Local Historians
David Smith
0 7134 5192 0

Maps for Local History
Paul Hindle
0 7134 5584 5

Photographs and Local History
George Oliver
0 7134 5679 5

Record Sources for Local History
Philip Riden
0 7134 5726 0

Researching the Country House
Elton/Harrison/Wark
0 7134 6440 2

Scottish Family History
David Moody
0 7134 5725 2

Scottish Local History
David Moody
0 7134 5221 8

Scottish Place-Names
W. F. H. Nicolaisen
0 7134 5234 X

Short History of Wales
A. H. Dodd
0 7134 1466 9

Thatchers and Thatching
Judy Nash
0 7134 6458 5